WAITING FOR
"SUPERMAN"

a participant° guide
MEDIA

WAITING FOR

"*SUPERMAN*"

How We Can Save
America's Failing Public Schools

Edited by

Karl Weber

PUBLICAFFAIRS
New York

Published in the United States by PublicAffairs™, a member of the
Perseus Books Group.

PublicAffairs books are available at special discounts for bulk purchases in the U.S.
by corporations, institutions, and other organizations. For more information, please
contact the Special Markets Department at the Perseus Books Group, 2300 Chestnut
Street, Suite 200, Philadelphia, PA 19103, call (800) 810–4145, ext. 5000, or e-mail
special.markets@perseusbooks.com.

Text set in 12.5-point Minion Pro

Library of Congress Cataloging-in-Publication Data
    Waiting for "Superman": how we can save America's failing public schools /
edited by Karl Weber.
        p. cm.
    Includes bibliographical references and index.
    ISBN 978-1-58648–927–4 (pbk. original) 1. Educational accountability—
Law and legislation—United States. 2. Education—Standards—United States.
3. Education—United States—Evaluation. 4. School improvement programs—
United States. 5. Educational equalization—United States.

LB2806.22.W35 2010
379.10973—dc22

                                                            2010026986

First Edition

10 9 8 7

CONTENTS

PART IV—ANTHONY

PART V—BIANCA

PART VI—DAISY

PART VII—WHAT YOU CAN DO

PROLOGUE

THE PROBLEM

A Nation Still At Risk

In 1966, the famous Coleman Report alerted the American people to the unfolding tragedy of a dysfunctional educational system. Funded by the U.S. Department of Commerce in response to the concerns about educational inequality raised by the civil rights movement, the Coleman Report highlighted the alarming extent to which students from low-income minority groups were falling behind their more fortunate counterparts, creating a nation with two separate and radically unequal educational systems.

Seventeen years later, the National Commission on Excellence in Education issued its report on the declining quality of American schools in general. Titled *A Nation At Risk: The Imperative for Educational Reform*, the report startled the nation with its warning of "a rising tide of mediocrity" in our schools and its grim declaration, "If an unfriendly foreign power had attempted to impose on America the mediocre educational performance that exists today, we might well have viewed it as an act of war."

More than four decades have passed since the publication of the Coleman Report, and almost three decades since *A Nation*

At Risk—decades of debate, dissension, finger-pointing, and confusion. School systems around the country have made countless attempts to improve the overall quality of education, pursuing a wide variety of strategies. Families and communities have turned to private schools, charter schools, magnet schools, parochial schools, home-schooling, and a series of other attempted remedies. Major national efforts such as the No Child Left Behind legislation spearheaded by President George W. Bush and Senator Edward M. Kennedy have been mounted. Hundreds of billions of dollars have been thrown at the problem. Yet in the aggregate, the problems the Coleman Report and *A Nation At Risk* identified have not been alleviated. In fact, by most measures, they have only gotten worse.

Here are just some of the damning statistics that illustrate how serious the problems with American education have become—and suggest some of the causes:

- Eight years after the passage of No Child Left Behind, the United States has four years left to reach the act's goal of 100 percent proficiency in math and reading—but most states currently hover around 20 percent or 30 percent proficiency.

- Among thirty developed countries, the United States is ranked twenty-fifth in math and twenty-first in science. When the comparison is restricted to the top 5 percent of students, the United States is ranked last.

- Barely half of African-American and Latino students graduate from high school. African-American students graduate at 51 percent, Latinos at 55 percent, while their white counterparts graduate at (a still lower than optimal) 76 percent.

- The economic costs of failing schools are enormous. For example, in Pennsylvania, 68 percent of state prison inmates are high school dropouts. The state spends $33,000 a year on each prisoner, and the total cost of the average prison term is $132,000. By contrast, the average private school costs $8,300 per student per year. So for the same amount, Pennsylvania could have sent a prison inmate to a private school from kindergarten through twelfth grade—and still had more than $24,000 left for college.

- Fifty years ago, only 20 percent of high school graduates expected to go to college. Most of those who did would become doctors, lawyers, engineers, clergymen, and top corporate executives. The next 20 percent were expected to go straight into skilled jobs as accountants, managers, technicians, or bureaucrats, while the bottom 60 percent would become workers on farms and in factories, in an economy where those occupations generally paid wages sufficient to support a family. Based on these numbers, a system of tracking or grouping by ability emerged that served American school systems reasonably well. Today most middle-class high schools still track their students in this manner, even though the economy now requires a much higher percentage of college graduates. The gap between what we need and what we are producing is large, and growing. In fact, by the year 2020, 123 million American jobs will be in high-skill/high-pay occupations, from computer programming to bioengineering, but only 50 million Americans will be qualified to fill them.

- The average college graduate earns 73 percent more than the average high school graduate in a lifetime. Based on this relationship, The Alliance for Excellent Education has estimated that the approximately 1.2 million students who should have graduated with the college class of 2008—but failed to do so—will cost the nation nearly $319 billion in lost income over the course of their lives.

- High school graduates on average live up to seven years longer than high school dropouts.

- In 1970, the United States produced 30 percent of the world's college graduates. Today it produces only 15 percent.

- At America's top 150 colleges, 90 percent of incoming freshmen come from families in the top half of U.S. annual income statistics.

- Since 1971, education spending in the United States has more than doubled from $4,300 per student to more than $9,000 per student (adjusted for inflation). Yet in that same time period, reading and math scores have remained flat in the United States, even as they have risen in virtually every other developed country.

- Teachers' unions, originally formed in the mid-nineteenth century, began as leading voices in the national movement for women's rights and the rights of all working people. Today they are also major political forces. Taken together, the two biggest teachers' unions, the National Education Association (NEA) and the American Federation of Teachers (AFT), are the nation's largest contributors to political campaigns. Over the past twenty years, they have given more than $55 million to congressional candidates and their parties, more than the Teamsters, the National Rifle Association, the AARP, the National Chamber of Commerce, or any other organization. More than 90 percent of this money goes to Democrats.

- As a profession, teachers enjoy some of the strongest protections of any group of workers. For example, in Illinois, 1 in 57 doctors loses his or her medical license, and 1 in 97 attorneys loses his or her law license, but only 1 teacher in 2,500 has ever lost his or her credentials.

- In New York state, disciplinary hearings for teachers last eight times longer than the average U.S. criminal case. The cost to the State of New York of teachers awaiting these hearings is $65 million a year.

- Recent research into teacher effectiveness demonstrates that the performance gap between the best teachers and the worst teachers is far greater than commonly supposed. On average, a teacher in the bottom quintile of effectiveness covers only 50 percent of the required curriculum in a school year, while a teacher in the top quintile covers 150 percent. Research reflects the cumulative impact of the difference on a group of students over multiple years: In Dallas, students who had three consecutive years of effective teachers improved their math test scores by 21 points, while students with three years of ineffective teachers fell 30 points behind.

- Teacher retention is a serious problem for many American school districts. By some estimates, approximately 40 percent of teachers leave the profession within five years of starting to teach, while 50 percent leave within six years. The problem is worst in the neediest school districts. Nationwide, 15.2 percent of teachers at high-poverty schools leave their schools annually, compared to 10.5 percent in low-poverty settings.

- As a result of the teacher retention challenge, 20 percent of teachers in high-poverty schools are inexperienced, compared with 11 percent in low-poverty schools; the figures are 21 percent in high-minority schools and 10 percent in low-minority schools.

Of course, statistics alone don't tell the story, and numbers isolated from a social, economic, and political context can be misleading and subject to abuse.

For example, experts disagree about the significance of teacher retention statistics. On average, more-experienced teachers produce better student results—but only on average. There are teachers with many years in the classroom who are mediocre at best, and some newcomers to the profession who are deeply gifted and able to produce superb outcomes almost from their first days on the job. Identifying the high performers, weeding out the low performers, and improving the work of those in the middle ranks is the big challenge—and as you'll read in this book, much progress has been made in developing tools to make this possible.

Others, especially advocates for teachers' unions, point to high rates of teacher turnover as an important corrective to what they consider misleading statistics about the tiny numbers of teachers who are removed from their jobs for incompetence. That relatively large numbers of teachers quit the profession within a few years indicates, they say, an important self-policing mechanism at work, with those unsuited to teaching choosing voluntary departures. But what both sides of this particular debate increasingly agree upon is that teacher performance matters, a lot; that the (relatively small) numbers of ineffective teachers should be moved out of the classroom; and that the many skilled and dedicated teachers already at work in our schools need the resources, training, rewards, and encouragement to continue and improve their efforts.

Statistics alone can tell us only so much. But almost thirty years after *A Nation At Risk*, it seems very clear that too many American schools are still failing. They are failing to prepare students adequately for higher education and for the challenging workplaces of the future; they are failing to produce the large numbers of high-skilled professionals our country will need to remain economically competitive; and they are, most egregiously, failing to provide students from ethnic and racial minorities, as well as the economically disadvantaged, with the intellectual tools they need to achieve their piece of the American dream. Our nation is already seriously stratified between haves and have-nots, the latter too often marked from birth and given little realistic chance of catching up. For the good of all Americans, that inequality must change—and education is the most obvious and natural place to make that change possible.

In their remarkable documentary *Waiting for "Superman,"* director Davis Guggenheim, producer Lesley Chilcott, and the talented team of artists and craftspeople who supported them have provided a moving, thoughtful, and inspiring contribution to the national debate that surrounds the issue of educational reform. This companion book, inspired by the film, attempts to offer its own contribution. Through the insights, experiences, and wisdom of many of America's leading experts on education, each with a unique and uniquely valuable perspective, we want to help inform the debate, clarify the issues, suggest how much has already been accomplished by today's most gifted school reformers, and illuminate the problems that continue to elude solution.

Perhaps most important, we hope to remind readers—whether they are students or teachers, parents or grandparents, policy makers or concerned citizens—that the cause of school reform is one that affects us all . . . and that redeeming the promise of a world-class education for *all* of our citizens is a cause worth working, and fighting, for.

PART I

THE FILM

PARTICIPANT MEDIA

presents

an ELECTRIC KINNEY FILMS production of

A FILM BY DAVIS GUGGENHEIM

WAITING FOR *"SUPERMAN"*

MUSIC BY

Christophe Beck

EDITED BY

Greg Finton, Jay Cassidy, A.C.E., Kim Roberts

CINEMATOGRAPHY BY

Erich Roland, Bob Richman

CO-PRODUCED BY

Eliza Hindmarch

EXECUTIVE PRODUCERS

Jeff Skoll, Diane Weyermann

WRITTEN BY

Davis Guggenheim and Billy Kimball

PRODUCED BY

Lesley Chilcott

DIRECTED BY

Davis Guggenheim

INTRODUCTION

Waiting for "Superman"—
The Story Behind the Movie

One of the saddest days of my life was when my mother told me *"Superman"* did not exist. Cause even in the depths of the ghetto you just thought he was coming. . . . She thought I was crying because it's like Santa Claus is not real. I was crying because no one was coming with enough power to save us.

—Geoffrey Canada, *Waiting for "Superman"*

Every morning, in big cities, suburbs, and small towns across America, parents send their children off to school with the highest of hopes. But a shocking number of students in the United States attend schools where they have virtually no chance of learning—failure factories likelier to produce dropouts than college graduates. And despite decades of well-intended reforms and huge sums of money spent on the problem, our public schools haven't improved markedly since the 1970s. Why? There is an answer. And it's not what you think.

Davis Guggenheim, director of *An Inconvenient Truth*, has now directed *Waiting for "Superman,"* a provocative and cogent examination of the crisis of public education in the United States told through multiple interlocking stories—from a handful of students and their families whose futures hang in the balance, to the educators and reformers trying to find real and lasting solutions within a dysfunctional system.

Tackling such politically radioactive topics as the power of teachers' unions and the entrenchment of school bureaucracies, Guggenheim reveals the invisible forces that have held back true education reform for decades.

At the dawn of the twentieth century, public education was a cornerstone of the American way of life. As millions of immigrant children arrived in the United States, public schools offered them the opportunity to participate in the American dream. In contrast to European educational models at the time, which reserved secondary schooling for children of the elite, Americans of all economic classes began to attend high school to prepare for white- and blue-collar jobs. With the passage of the GI Bill after World War II, higher education was opened up to a broader group than ever before.

In the 1950s, America's public schools were brimming with the promise of unlimited possibilities for the baby boomers. But that sense of potential didn't extend to everyone. Starting with the U.S. Supreme Court case *Brown v. Board of Education* in 1954, public schools became a key battlefield in the fight for equality, as school segregation was gradually and often violently dismantled. Schools also became a sphere for playing out Cold War anxieties, as the USSR's launch of the space satellite *Sputnik* inspired a wave of investment in America's would-be scientists and engineers.

By the 1970s, the United States was granting a better education to a larger percentage of its population than most of the rest of the world. Two hundred years after the Declaration of Independence, the United States was well on its way to equipping its children—regardless of their race, gender, or social class—for stewardship of a democracy.

In the thirty years since then, however, the steady progress of the American education system has ground to a halt. As countries in the rest of the world have continued to advance, U.S. reading and math scores have frozen in place. For poor and minority students, the outlook is particularly bleak. The 1983 report *A Nation At Risk* asserted that the American public education system was in crisis. And yet wave after wave of reform and a doubling of per pupil spending have made no apparent impact on student achievement.

By the time President George W. Bush and Senator Ted Kennedy pushed the No Child Left Behind Act (NCLB) to passage in 2001, most Americans agreed that the public education system was broken, and many felt it was beyond repair. The NCLB Act required states to conduct standardized tests in reading and math in certain grades, and emphasized teacher quality. Although NCLB's success has been widely questioned and the federal government has failed to fully fund some of its mandates, one of the by-products of the legislation was the emergence of hard data on which schools were succeeding and which were failing.

In some troubled neighborhoods, diamonds emerged, as a new generation of reformers proved change really was possible. In 2010, families are flocking to those few exemplary public schools, often competing in lotteries for admittance. Only a small fraction of them will get in. In other neighborhoods, families don't even have a lottery on which to pin their hopes.

• • •

In 1999, filmmaker Davis Guggenheim completed his first documentary feature, *The First Year*, a chronicle of the experiences of a group of novice public school teachers in charge of their classrooms for the very first time. In the decade that followed, Guggenheim went on to make films on a variety of topics, including the 2006 Oscar-winning hit *An Inconvenient Truth*, which started a worldwide conversation about climate change.

But it was circumstances in his own family that inspired him to revisit the subject of education. As a father of three, the director found his ideals about public schooling bumping up against the hard reality of his own family's best interests. Guggenheim looked up the test scores of his neighborhood school in Venice, California. "They were so damning," he says, "I thought, 'I can't do this.' My feelings about public education didn't matter as much as my fear of sending my kids to a failing school. And so, every morning, betraying the ideals I thought I lived by, I drive past three public schools as I take my kids to a private school." *Waiting for "Superman"* became a personal journey for Guggenheim, allowing the director to grapple with these issues and their implications for other families, those with fewer options.

Ten years after making *The First Year*, Guggenheim found the landscape dramatically changed. "In 1999 the problems in our public schools felt hopeless," he says. "Now there are reformers who are defying the odds and proving that it's possible to have an outstanding school in a troubled neighborhood." Even in struggling communities, we now have model public schools that send 90 percent of their students to college.

And yet, for too many neighborhoods in America, the public schools have been failing even with the well-intended reforms. Guggenheim documents the political forces that conspire to keep educators from replicating successful reforms on a grander scale and within the system. As a result, there aren't enough spaces at good public schools for all the children who want to attend them. Many of the country's best schools admit students in the fairest way they can—by lottery. In heartbreaking detail, Guggenheim shows how the public school lottery process is one with real winners and losers, as some children get a chance at a better life and many more are left . . . waiting.

In 2008, Guggenheim and producer Lesley Chilcott set out to find families participating in the public school lottery process, documenting their journeys from failing neighborhood schools to—the families hope—better opportunities. "We were looking for a way to communicate the gravity of our education problem when we learned about the lotteries," says Chilcott. "It just seemed so wrong—really the opposite of what America stands for. You can go to the store and there are seven different kinds of peanut butter to choose from, but you don't get to choose your school? And when there is a good school available to you, the way you get in is determined by a bouncing ball in a cage?"

Through school admissions officials and interviews conducted at lottery information sessions, the filmmakers collected information about twenty families with compelling and varied stories before ultimately narrowing down that number to the five in the film: Anthony, a Washington, D.C., fifth grader orphaned by drugs; Bianca, a Harlem kindergartner whose mom is stretched to the limit paying her Catholic school tuition; Daisy, an East Los Angeles fifth grader whose parents didn't finish high school; Emily, a middle-class Silicon Valley eighth grader trying to stay off the dead-end remedial track; and Francisco, a Bronx first grader who has already been denied entrance to seven charter schools and has just one more chance to get out of his overcrowded neighborhood school.

Over the course of a year, they spent multiple days with those parents and children at locations in New York City, Washington, D.C., and Northern and Southern California. "We ended up with a diverse mix of families from different cities, and with different concerns," Chilcott says. "But what was interesting was what they had in common: Every parent was working for the sake of their kids to make sure they had a better education."

At their offices, Guggenheim and Chilcott also hosted informal lunches for various educational experts of all backgrounds and disciplines, peppering the meetings with questions that helped the filmmakers find the thinkers and innovators at the leading edge of education. They broached the taboo topics of public school reform with such people as Washington, D.C., Schools chancellor Michelle Rhee, Harlem Children's Zone president and CEO Geoffrey Canada, and Stanford University senior fellow Eric Hanushek. "You start to realize that we do know what the problems are," Chilcott says. "And there *are* people who know how to fix them."

With *Waiting for "Superman,"* Guggenheim wanted to take the conversation beyond staid policy discussions and into the subjects no one wanted to talk about, what he calls the "uncomfortable truths" about public education. The film explores ugly industry realities such as the "dance of the lemons," when principals can't fire bad teachers, and so instead transfer them to another school where they become that principal's problem; the "rubber rooms," where suspended teachers wait for a hearing, often kept on salary for years, doing nothing; and the inability of school districts to reward great teachers due to their stifling union contracts. "As much as politicians, reformers, and the press know what the real problems are, they're not going to talk about them," Guggenheim says. "They're politically deadly. But the only way we're going to address this crisis is if these uncomfortable truths are spoken out loud. And the only person who can say it is someone independent of the system, like maybe a documentary filmmaker.

"For forty years we've poured money into the system and it hasn't worked, and we've poured great people with the best intentions into the system and it hasn't worked," he continues. "So my feeling was, 'Why don't we make a movie about the invisible forces that are keeping it from working?' And if we show the real human cost of the dysfunction—the kids and mothers and fathers fighting for them—then maybe people will be outraged enough to demand real change."

One of the revelations of *Waiting for "Superman"* is the extent of the crisis in ostensibly good suburban schools. One student profiled in the film, Emily, is slated to attend a well-regarded Silicon Valley high school that turns out to graduate only 65 percent of its freshmen. "When it comes to failing schools, it's not just 'those kids,' as upper-middle-class people might say," says Chilcott. "We've got a crisis at every income level and every type of school. One of the results of our continuing to accept this present system is that we're not producing scientists and engineers fast enough to keep pace with the rest of the world."

As in *An Inconvenient Truth*, Guggenheim and Chilcott found that raw data, used in context, would help convey the depth of the crisis. After collecting and synthesizing reams of research, the filmmakers vetted every statistic through a group of educators and experts. Through vivid and often whimsical animations by Brooklyn, New York, animation house Awesome + Modest, they were able to illustrate the data with clarity and emotion.

For all its complexity, *Waiting for "Superman"* came together relatively quickly. Guggenheim and Participant Media had forged a strong relationship on *An Inconvenient Truth*, and it seemed natural to reteam for a film on a shared passion—illuminating the crisis in public education. The filmmakers wrote a treatment in early 2008 and began shooting later that year. During editing, they made an unusual choice for a documentary and decided to include Guggenheim's interview questions. "Usually you do everything you can to cut out a person's questions," Guggenheim explains. "But we wanted to let the audience in on that relationship between me searching for some answers and the person I'm interviewing."

Six-time Grammy Award–winning recording artist, concert performer, and philanthropist John Legend composed the heart-stirring anthem "Shine" for the movie's closing credits. Legend's collaboration with the filmmakers came about serendipitously. The singer-songwriter, who has long been committed to making a difference in the lives of others and whose Show Me Campaign uses education to break the cycle of poverty, was considering producing a documentary about public education. Legend's manager just happened to approach Guggenheim about directing it. Guggenheim stopped him and said, "I'm actually halfway through making that movie." The lucky meeting resulted in a song that both moves and mobilizes any listener who cares about children. "'Shine' manages to say musically everything that we wanted to say in this film but couldn't," Guggenheim says. "The first time I heard it, I cried."

Waiting for "Superman" makes clear that the noble vision of America's public schools is attainable. All children can learn and all neighborhoods can have good schools. All that is lacking is a country of moms and dads armed with the truth, and the conviction to change it. "The big idea of what America is about is at stake," Guggenheim says. "That every kid can have a chance. And right now, at this very moment, it's possible to fix it."

Voices from *Waiting for "Superman"*

"I want to go to college and get an education. Because if I have kids, I want kids to be in this environment. Like around here. Like, I mean, I want my kids to have better than I had."

—Anthony, fifth grader, Washington, D.C.

"There's this unbelievable willingness to turn a blind eye to the injustices that are happening to kids every single day in our schools in the name of harmony amongst adults."

"The question is, do we have the fortitude that it would take as a city and as a country to make the difficult decisions that would be necessary?"

"You wake up every morning and you know that 46,000 kids are counting on you. And that most of them are getting a really crappy education right now and you have the ability to do something about that."

—Michelle Rhee, Washington, D.C., Schools chancellor

"Twenty-five years ago, there was no proof that something else worked. Well, now we know what works. We know that it's just a lie that disadvantaged kids can't learn. We know that if you apply the right accountability standards you can get fabulous results. So why would we do something else?"

"This whole collection of people, which is sometimes called the Blob, like out of some horror movie, has been an impediment to reform. No individual is necessarily to blame but collectively they are the Goliath of the system."

"Nowadays if you don't go to college you're kind of screwed in America. And America's kind of screwed."

—*Jonathan Alter*, Newsweek *senior editor*

"I don't care what I have to do. I don't care how many jobs I have to obtain, but she will go to college and there's just no second-guessing on that one. You go to college, you learn, you get your education, and you don't get a job— you get a career. There's a difference."

—*Nakia, mother of Bianca, kindergartner, Harlem*

"We basically know which students are going to drop out in the next five years. We know which schools they go to and with just a little bit of digging we can see them raising their hands and saying 'help.'"

—*Robert Balfanz, Johns Hopkins University*

"I kept running into this issue of, 'Hey, you know what, I don't think we can do anything unless we deal with the unions.' 'No, no, that's off the table.' 'You can't even bring it up?' 'No.' 'Why can't you even talk about . . . ' 'No. Because it's off the table.' The mayors didn't want to talk about it, the folks at the statehouses, the governor, no one wanted to bring this up."

"When you see a great teacher you are seeing a work of art. You're seeing a master and it is as, I think, as unbeliev-able as seeing a great athlete or seeing a great musician."

—*Geoffrey Canada, president and CEO*
of the Harlem Children's Zone

"If in fact we could just eliminate the bottom 6 to 10 percent of our teachers and replace them with an average teacher, we could bring the average U.S. student up to the level of Finland, which is at the top of the world today."

—*Eric Hanushek, Stanford University*

"We cannot sustain an economy based on innovation un-less we have citizens well educated in math, science, and engineering. If we fail at this, we won't be able to compete in the global economy. How strong the country is twenty years from now and how equitable the country is twenty years from now will be largely driven by this issue."

—*Bill Gates, co-chair and trustee,*
Bill & Melinda Gates Foundation; chairman, Microsoft Corp.

"I won't give up on my kids. There's just so many different parents out there that want so much for their children."

—*Mari, mother of Francisco, first grader, the Bronx*

"We have often been called a special interest and I will never apologize for that because our special interests are the students we teach. They are worth fighting for with every weapon in our arsenal."

—Randi Weingarten,
American Federation of Teachers president

"Daisy, cross your fingers."

—Jose, father of Daisy, fifth grader,
awaiting the results of a school lottery in L.A.

The Making of
Waiting for "Superman"

Davis Guggenheim

Davis Guggenheim is a critically acclaimed, Academy Award–winning director and producer whose early work includes many television dramas, such as *Deadwood*, *NYPD Blue*, and *24*. He transitioned into directing nonfiction films with *The First Year*, which aired on PBS in 2001 and won a Peabody Award. *An Inconvenient Truth*, featuring former vice president Al Gore, was theatrically distributed by Paramount in 2006 and won an Academy Award for Best Documentary. *It Might Get Loud*, featuring Jimmy Page, The Edge, and Jack White, was theatrically distributed by Sony Pictures Classics in 2009. Guggenheim also directed Barack Obama's biographical film for the 2008 Democratic National Convention, as well as Obama's thirty-minute prime-time infomercial.

Guggenheim's latest film, *Waiting for "Superman,"* has been given theatrical distribution by Paramount. It premiered at the 2010 Sundance Film Festival and took home the Best U.S. Documentary Audience Award.

Iused to find it disturbing; now I just find it amusing—that stare I get when I tell people that my next film is about the public education system. Even the most decent people retreat to a polite smile and fumble for something nice to say that basically amounts to "Oh, that's so noble." In reality, they're saying, "Good luck getting people to see that one."

The sad truth is this response is understandable. The story of public education has been told many times over the past forty years, and often very movingly. But on the whole, most people feel it's a static and hopeless story. The dark voices inside people's heads say, "Why open my heart to a problem that is confusing and never seems to get any better?" or, "We've heard all the sob stories before, and all we've accomplished is to get depressed and feel guilty."

That is why when Diane Weyerman called from Participant Media asking if I wanted to make a movie on the current state of public education in America, I said I wasn't interested. I was flattered by the offer, but I told her I didn't think it could be done—at least not in a way that would make a real difference. The issue was so complex, it was a storyteller's quagmire.

That was in August 2007. A month later, I heard the dark voices speaking—inside my own head. It was back-to-school week, and I was driving the familiar route past three public schools to my kids' private school. Years earlier my wife and I had researched our neighborhood public school and discovered it wasn't up to snuff. So we did what other parents who can afford it did: We opened up our wallets and paid lots of money so that our kids could get a great education. But today the voice was strong and insistent: "You've found a great school for your kids—but is that enough? You've pulled your kids from the system and turned your back on the problem. Your kids will be okay, but what about other people's children?" That last question was the worst one of all—the one I couldn't seem to shake.

"Other people's children"—that phrase kept echoing in my head like a challenge. How do I get people to care as much about other people's children as they do their own? Without making a decision, it was decided. And I had no choice. I was going to try again to tell this story, even though I had no clue how.

• • •

Everything I learned about filmmaking came from my father, Charles Guggenheim, who made great documentaries from the 1960s through the 1990s. Dad directed a whole series of films with strong social justice content—including two documentaries about American education: one called *Children Without* (1964), which dealt with kids growing up in the Detroit projects, and another called *High Schools* (1984), based on the famous report by Dr. Ernest L. Boyer on the state of American schools.

I grew up watching Dad work, literally waking up to the sound of his Moviola grinding film as he edited it in our living room. I spent my youth learning from him about filmmaking and seeing the power of movies at work in promoting social change and the quest for justice.

It was fascinating for me to grow up in Washington, D.C., where my dad did most of his work, in a home filled with amazing people up to and including Robert F. Kennedy, whose presidential campaign my father worked on—in fact, Dad's memorial film about Bobby earned a twenty-minute standing ovation at the 1968 Democratic National Convention and went on to win an Oscar. I got to meet so many people dedicated to world-changing missions, such as eradicating poverty, ending pollution, reversing racial discrimination, and providing every kid with a fine education. As a filmmaker, my father was immersed in this work. And while he was admired in filmmaking circles for his accomplishments, he wasn't a celebrity. Few recognized the slender man riding his bike to work every day. But he won four Academy Awards, was nominated for twelve more—and was my greatest teacher.

I helped my dad on some of his pictures, and after I graduated from Brown, he said, "Come work for me." It was a tempting offer, but after thinking it over, I realized that I couldn't accept. You don't inherit a film company. If you're going to be a filmmaker, you have to break out on your own. So I moved to Hollywood with the goal of becoming a successful mainstream director rather than a specialist in documentaries. I guess that was my version of the step toward independence that every young person needs to take at some point.

I had several jobs in the movie business in the 1990s, and I was working my way up the ladder as a producer when I finally hooked into a script that I really loved and had a special feeling for. I discovered and developed it and sold it to Warner Brothers, with me attached as director. It was called *Training Day*. I fought very hard to get Denzel Washington into it, and I finally convinced everyone to offer it to him. And he said yes—but not with Davis directing. So I was fired from my own movie, without any fanfare and certainly with no recourse.

I never learned for sure why Denzel didn't want me on the picture. Maybe he wanted someone with more "street cred" to handle a gritty urban story like *Training Day*. (It was eventually directed by Antoine Fuqua, and won Denzel the Academy Award for Best Actor in 2001.) But whatever the reason for my dismissal, it left me brokenhearted and disillusioned with Hollywood.

And as it turned out, this became the impetus for me to go back to my father's roots in the world of documentaries. At the same time I was developing *Training Day*, I'd been thinking about making a documentary about a group of teachers I'd read about who inspired me deeply. Education was just becoming a personal issue for me; I had a child, just five or six months old, several years away from going to school himself. But the story of these teachers, working in Los Angeles public schools with the support of a brand-new, very ambitious educational program called Teach For America, was one that gripped me.

These young teachers going into inner-city schools reminded me of my dad's era. When I heard Wendy Kopp, founder of Teach For America, speak about her idea for revitalizing public schools through a new kind of "domestic Peace Corps" program and infusing them with the energy of bright young people, it felt as if the spirit of the sixties was being reborn—that feeling of idealism, hope, and commitment to making the world a better place. So this concept touched me in a lot of ways and made me say, "This is a story that needs to be told."

I spent a year following those five young teachers through their first year in the classroom, and the result was my first documentary, *The First Year*.

As you can imagine, I was pretty nervous when my dad attended an early screening of *The First Year* in Washington, D.C. There was no critic in the world whose opinion of the movie was more important to me. In the middle of the show, I ducked out of the theater to take a walk—something I often do during screenings because, as the director, I've seen the footage so many times before. On my way out, I caught a glimpse of my father in the back of the room, pacing and looking at the screen, a little nervous but totally absorbed, maybe the way Archie Manning watches Peyton or Eli quarterbacking an NFL game. He was watching his son and what he'd done with his first documentary. Dad didn't see me, but I could see him. I don't know exactly what he was thinking, but his eyes were bright with energy, and he was engaged. I think he was proud.

That was one of the great moments of my life.

I was very happy with *The First Year*, and all of us who worked on it were very excited when it premiered on PBS in the fall of 2001. Meryl Streep introduced the broadcast, and we got a lot of great comments and compliments about it. (It ultimately won a Peabody Award.) But then, four days after the premiere, 9/11 came. And suddenly nobody seemed to be talking or thinking about the problems of public education.

At the time, of course, we were all overwhelmed by the trauma of the terrorist attacks. So the sense of disappointment about our film didn't hit until later. But the disappointment was very real. When you make a film about a social problem, you hope to have an impact on the national conversation. Thanks to this accident of timing, that wasn't possible.

But timing wasn't the only problem. In reflecting afterward on *The First Year*, I realized that it wasn't doing what a documentary film should do. It captured the personal challenges of teaching and the tremendous challenges faced by students and teachers in a troubled school district. But those things have been shown in movies made over the past few decades. We weren't really breaking new ground. The film needed to have a stronger voice and a stronger point of view.

I spent the next few years working on a range of dramatic projects, including episodes of *24* and *Deadwood*. But the insights into nonfiction moviemaking that I'd gleaned from *The First Year* were percolating in the back of my mind.

So when the opportunity arose to work on *An Inconvenient Truth* with former vice president Al Gore, I was ready for an artistic breakthrough which ultimately came from an unlikely place—two different discoveries I made.

The first actually goes back to a key lesson my father taught me. He always said that people are interested in people, and when they go to a movie, no matter how interesting and how important the topic of your movie is, they stay and watch because they're invested in the stories of people you've captured on film. The biggest mistake most documentaries make is to forget this simple truth. For *An Inconvenient Truth*, we had to figure out a new way of introducing that quality of personal narrative into a scientific slide show—and in the process, we discovered an approach that ultimately shaped *Waiting for "Superman."*

The project that became *An Inconvenient Truth* originated when Laurie David and Lawrence Bender came to me and said, "We have this idea for a movie based on a slide show about global warming that Al Gore gives." My first reaction was that this was a terrible idea—in fact, I spent two hours trying to talk them out of it. But then I saw Al's slide show, and it was amazing. It was just the unedited slide show—twice as long as what you see in the movie, and very raw—but it was so powerfully compelling that I said, "We have to make this movie because it's too important not to get this information out there."

The problem was that I had no idea how to make it work as a film.

Al's slide show, while intellectually fascinating, didn't have that essential thing my father had taught me about. It didn't have the personal hook that every movie needs. And so I realized I had to go beyond the topic of global warming by including a series of intensely personal stories about Al Gore—about his discovery of the inspiring teacher Roger Revelle, about his frustrating quest to educate Congress on the problem of climate change, about the Gore family's tobacco farm and the death of Al's sister from lung cancer, about the near-death of Al's son in a car crash, and other very personal anecdotes.

A lot of people thought this approach was crazy. They said out loud what I was asking myself: "How are you going to inject this personal story line into a slide show?" But my instinct told me that this was the way to go—even if I didn't know how to do it.

So I started to build what I called "little movies"—short sequences showing things like Al walking through an airport late at night, alone, pulling his luggage behind him, or Al visiting the tobacco farm his family once ran and reflecting on their tragic relationship with that deadly crop. I didn't know whether these little movies would work. In fact, some people watched the finished film and strongly recommended that I take them out. Al himself wasn't so sure it was relevant to bring in the personal side of the story—he later joked that he felt as if he was in *Kill Al Part III.*

But I stuck with the idea. I knew we needed some way to give people a personal entrée into the story—something you could get from Al's personal presence when attending a slide show in an auditorium but that would be lacking from a filmed version of the presentation.

I remember early in the filmmaking process saying to Al, "You're Cassandra. You can see and understand this terrible and alarming truth, yet you're cursed with the fact that no one will listen to you." Al quickly replied, "No, no, no, that is not true." It's understandable that Al didn't want to see it that way. But there was something incredible and noble about this quest of his, especially in the context of that historical moment in time. The 2000 election was still fresh in everyone's mind, George W. Bush's presidency was starting to tank, and there was a moment when millions of Americans were ready to rediscover Al Gore, this public figure whom we all thought we understood, but didn't. I began to see in Al's personal narrative the elements of a redemption story.

Now in the end, the personal narrative about Al Gore ended up being only a third of *An Inconvenient Truth,* but I think it is what hooks you in. In fact, when people see the movie, they often react as if they are getting to know Al Gore for the first time. Many say, "Why didn't I see that Al Gore during the 2000 campaign?"

Of course, it's easy in retrospect to describe the sequence of events as if I had a master plan from the very beginning. The truth is, the path to finding a story that worked was not a straight one. It was filled with anxiety and shadowed by the voices of the naysayers, none more convincing than the ones inside my own head. Truthfully, the final product emerged less from a thought-out design than from necessity.

An Inconvenient Truth works because of the combination of disparate elements. We had Al's slide show that was so compelling, while in the other scenes we went intensely off-camera, only hearing Al's voice as he recalled some deeply emotional memories, giving us a glimpse of the human being behind the cause. Told more traditionally, these personal stories would have featured Al on camera, but because the slide show featured Al talking the entire time, it felt more impactful to merely hear his voice in the personal sequences.

At the time, the decision making felt more desperate than thoughtful. I never would have done it this way if I hadn't had to. But what I discovered along the way was a different kind of storytelling—a startling interplay between the audience getting really important information that helps them understand an issue that is shocking and powerful, and an intensely personal narrative that makes the issue even more engaging.

To think of it differently, there was another, more traditional way we could have tried to personalize the movie. We could have sought to dramatize the problem of global warming by showing people whose lives are being affected by it. We could have gone to talk to the farmer in Vermont whose livelihood has changed, or the villager in Bangladesh whose farm has been flooded, or the people in New Orleans whose homes have been destroyed by hurricanes or rising sea levels. It would have been a very different movie, and maybe it would have worked. But somehow I was drawn to Al's story and the fact that he saw this problem so vividly and took it so much to heart.

Out of desperation I followed my instinct, and out of it came something that I couldn't possibly have conjured up. It's interesting—many people who had been following the issue of global warming for years could have responded to *An Inconvenient Truth* with a big yawn, saying, "I've seen all this information before." But they'd never seen it the way Al Gore presented it, and they'd certainly never seen it in the framework of one man's personal quest to get people to understand what was inside his head.

• • •

Three years later, I was celebrating having my new movie "greenlit" by Participant Media, the same company that had financed *An Inconvenient Truth*. Jim Berk, the new CEO of Participant, had been a public school principal. He was passionate about public education and was hoping I could create another big success with this film. But my joy at getting my next gig turned dark rather quickly as I thought about the huge challenge of getting people to really pay attention to this complicated, seemingly insoluble social problem.

But I'd agreed to do the movie and I'd taken the money—so there was no turning back. Having promised Participant, and the world, that I knew where I was going, I had to figure out what I actually wanted to do and how to do it.

Looking back, there are plenty of films that present intensely personal stories about students and teachers, including my father's and my own, *The First Year*. There are also movies that offer very thorough, intellectual, programmatic analyses of the educational system and why our schools are failing. But no one had done a movie that combines both approaches and uses that hybrid structure to take audiences to a really new place.

So I decided to do something rather radical, following the accidental plan of *An Inconvenient Truth*. I decided to make two different movies, oppositional in nature, looking at the school system from two very different angles, and then combine them.

I mean this very literally. In fact, three weeks before we were to show our cut of *Waiting for "Superman"* to the Sundance Film Festival, I had two movies that were in two different rooms on two different editing machines—completely separate movies. One captured five kids' stories in a movie that might be called *Other People's Children*, since it focused on the plight of these kids whom I hoped the audience would grow to care about as much as their own and who have to rely on the luck of a bouncing ball to determine whether they will attend a decent school. The other film was the story of why our educational system has stopped working—the bureaucracy, the dysfunctional incentives, the entrenched power of the unions, and so on. For tone purposes, I labeled this film with the working title *The Folly of the Adults*.

I worked for a year and a half filming those two separate movies and editing them so they would work in isolation—beginning, middle, and end. And then finally, three weeks before submitting to Sundance, we cut them together.

During much of this process, many of my most trusted friends and advisers were saying, "You're out of your mind." Even Lesley Chilcott, my producer and business partner, who understood exactly what I was trying to do, was getting nervous as the months passed, saying, "It's time to cut the movies together." But I kept saying, "They're not ready yet. They have to work in isolation, each as its own story, before we cut them together," and I refused to think about combining them until that first stage of the process was really completed.

Understand, I even refused to consider *how* and *where* we might combine the two separate pictures. Sometimes one of the editors would say, "Well, don't you think you should cut from this scene about one of the kids to this scene from the other film? Wouldn't that make a great juxtaposition?" I would always reply, "I don't even want to think about where the two pictures will meet. I just want to make them work as separate movies."

This was based on my experience with *An Inconvenient Truth*. When editor Jay Cassidy and I cut together the slide show and the little movies about Al Gore, I would say things like, "Well, we'll cut to Roger Revelle when Al's talking about such and such a topic," looking for logical, natural connections among ideas and themes. That's the traditional way of planning cuts. But the funny thing is that in the final movie, those weren't the most powerful links. Jay and I discovered that the most powerful links were where we intercut scenes that appeared to have very little to do with each other.

Now, working on *Waiting for "Superman,"* Jay and his fellow editors Greg Finton and Kimberly Roberts began to experiment with these strong "collision" cuts. We deliberately chose to create "random" cuts between the two independent movies. So when we jump from the problems of young Anthony and his grandmother trying to find a decent school in Washington, D.C., to President Bush giving a speech about his No Child Left Behind legislation, the big collision of ideas that results has an effect that I'd never seen before. In storytelling terms, I found that, surprisingly often, one plus one equals three—the unexpected connections between two unrelated ideas produce an amazing resonance that deepens the audience's experience in a way that's hard to describe.

By contrast, going back to *The First Year*, which is a much more traditional documentary, what's powerful about that movie is the experience of spending a year immersed in the lives of a group of young teachers and the tremendous challenges they face. It works very well on its own terms. But what you lose is the larger social, historical, and political context. Why is teaching so hard? Why are these kids coming into the classroom with such enormous deficits? Why is the educational system so blind to the needs of teachers? I came to realize that a film has to start to answer those questions, yet somehow shouldn't avoid losing the intimacy of a personal experience. So why not address both goals and let the two collide in the finished film?

As we cut the two films together, the strategy started to pay off. The emotional story of *Other People's Children* became more heartbreaking and real in contrast to the frustrating and ridiculous story of *The Folly of the Adults*—and vice versa.

This "illumination by collision" is at work throughout *Waiting for "Superman."* For example, there's a scene early in the film where we see Anthony walking by John Philip Sousa High School, where he's scheduled to go the following year. We have already learned that if Anthony goes there and performs like most of his classmates, by the time he finishes he will be three years below grade level in all his major subjects. Then the film cuts right to Michelle Rhee, the District of Columbia's superintendent of schools, saying, "Most of the kids in my city are getting a crappy education." Through that juxtaposition, the personal story of Anthony is immediately amplified into a picture of an entire system, and even an entire society, in crisis.

In other cases, we do the opposite—we start with the big picture and then cut to the personal story. For example, we have a scene in which we discuss how teacher tenure is making it harder for schools to improve the quality of their faculty and how teachers' unions are standing in the way of reform. And then we cut to Daisy, talking in her bright-eyed, idealistic way about her aspiration to someday be a doctor, and you suddenly understand not only how dysfunctional the system is but also how it affects these real-life kids you've come to care so much about.

As filmmakers, we're working both the brain and the heart. And this system of having two very different movies colliding in a single film feels to me like a powerful way to achieve that.

Ultimately, of course, these two worlds come together at the charter-school lottery, which is almost the final scene of the movie. We follow a kid showing up at the gymnasium with his grandmother to see his educational future determined by the bounce of a ball in a cage. It's the ultimate, surrealistic expression of the folly of the adults—that we allow a child's future to be a matter of sheer chance. And in that lottery sequence we see how the folly of the adults and the heartbreak of the kids come together in this very painful way.

It's not an effect I planned in advance—but it's there, and to me, when I watch it, it's devastating . . . another example of the power of film—to help you see things that might otherwise be invisible.

• • •

The second discovery that helped create the breakthrough we needed was about how documentaries, in my mind at least, have needed to shift in voice and tone to reach today's audiences.

Back in the 1960s and '70s, when making a social justice documentary, it was enough to take a camera into an unfamiliar place and show viewers the way things are. I'm thinking of classics like *Harvest of Shame*, the CBS News documentary about the plight of migrant farmworkers, or films like my dad's short features about the civil rights movement, *A Time for Justice* and *Nine from Little Rock*. It seems as though in those days, simply revealing to people the evils and injustices of the world could spark outrage and spur people to respond with action. The civil rights, environmental, antiwar, and feminist movements of that era were all fueled, in part, by the work of socially concerned filmmakers who educated a generation of Americans about the problems our society had been ignoring for too long.

Today, I think, a lot has changed. Several generations have passed, and cameras show us everything now. With the advent of twenty-four-hour cable news, the spread of tabloid journalism in both print and visual forms, and the rise of the Internet, we've become accustomed to seeing anything and everything on screens in front of us, from the terror of 9/11 and the horrors of Abu Ghraib to the devastation caused by Hurricane Katrina. As a result, we've become somewhat immune to the sorts of heart-tugging images that galvanized a nation thirty or forty years ago.

In addition, when it comes to the specific topic of public schools, the sense of cynicism and hopelessness is widespread. Most people won't say it in so many words, but the reaction of a lot of people to the problems of education in this country is something like, "Oh, I know that story and I know it's terrible, but there's nothing we can do about it." The sense of hopelessness induces a kind of indifference. People don't want to suffer the discomfort, even pain, of recognizing how serious the problem is when they believe they can't do anything about it. And so they turn off their receptors—or worse, their hearts—and ignore the topic.

This problem of breaking through the huge disconnect between an audience that could care, should care, and wants to care, but doesn't, was my biggest challenge when working on *Waiting for "Superman."*

Part of the solution, I think, is figuring out how to speak to the darker voices in people's heads. Those darker voices are the ones I evoke when I say in the movie, as I drive by public schools in run-down neighborhoods, that it's easy to think that maybe "those kids simply can't learn."

(There are a lot of shots in the movie about "driving by" failed schools. I kept being drawn to the real-life image of driving my family by the three public schools between our home and our private school. It's a metaphor for what we all do. We know there's a problem with American schools, and we feel bad about it, but we drive by and try to ignore it because we think it's unfixable.)

We all have those darker voices inside us. For instance, I have a mental block on problems such as the devastation from the earthquake in Haiti and the genocide in Darfur. I know about these problems, they disturb me, and maybe I donate a little money here and there to help out, but I don't want to engage the problems emotionally because they're so terrible and they seem too overwhelming. So when I see the article in the *New York Times*, rather than read it, I turn the page.

And as I worked on the movie, I was always struggling with the question: How will we keep people from turning the page? I didn't want to spend two years of my life struggling to make a movie that would fail to drive a real spike into people's consciousness.

One way we try to reach people is by appealing to their practical side, to their self-interest. There's a very carefully chosen moment, late in the movie, when I ask, "What happens when we fail a kid? What happens over time?" That question is at the heart of the movie, but the audience isn't ready to hear it until they've realized that this issue isn't just about people in need. It affects all of us in all sorts of ways—the health of the country, the future of our economy, even the price of your home. The complex story we paint in the first two-thirds of the movie is designed to reveal those connections, so when we ask the key question, the audience is ready for a shock of revelation.

It's mysterious to most people why the schools have been failing for so long. So we try to unravel what has made the problem so intractable by examining the political and systemic dysfunctions that have made it so difficult for well-meaning people to do the right thing, and that have created all kinds of crazy incentives for political leaders and union leaders and parents' organizations and taxpayers' groups to behave in ways that have complicated the situation rather than leading to the solutions that everyone, deep inside, really wants. Not until we untangle this mystery for people will they be ready to connect to the issue, and maybe invest in the solution.

From the beginning, I wanted to try to use humor in the movie. In *An Inconvenient Truth*, we had struggled with a kind of compassion fatigue. Audiences would grow exhausted trying to absorb all the data or feel overwhelmed with how heavy the subject matter became, and we noticed that even the smallest joke would have a huge effect in recharging people's emotional capacity.

In making *Waiting for "Superman,"* for the first time I enlisted the help of a writer, Billy Kimble, who could write deeply on complicated subjects and also do it with subtle and searing humor. One breakthrough moment was when we came across the fact that U.S. students rank far behind other advanced nations in academic achievement—ranked in the twenties in such subjects as math and science—but we come in at the very top in one area: self-confidence! In other words, American students don't know their algebra or their chemistry, but they sure as heck *think* they do! Billy had the idea of cutting to YouTube footage of daredevil American kids trying ambitious but absurd jumps with their bikes—and crashing. It's a non sequitur, and frankly I didn't think it would work, but the juxtaposition is so painfully ironic, and so revealing of our problems as a nation, that people can't help but laugh when they see it—at the same time they get angry at the complacency that has allowed us to reach this pathetic state.

So all these filmmaking techniques—appealing to people's practicality, their curiosity, and their sense of humor—were deliberately chosen to send a message to audiences that this is not the old-fashioned kind of documentary that only liberals (or so the cliché holds) used to watch decades ago. We're telling viewers, "We respect the position you're in. We know you suffer from empathy overload, that you've seen pictures of devastation and injustice and suffering a million times before. So we're not going to go into a school and point the cameras at leaking ceiling tiles and empty bookshelves and poor kids crying about their situation. We're going to go much further and talk about the dysfunction in a new way, in an analytical way, a humorous way, an ironic way. It's not about making you feel guilty—it's about making you think, and maybe, after all that, opening your heart and rousing you to action."

• • •

There was a moment when I was tempted to give up on the movie due to a crisis of conscience over how to handle the teachers' unions. The problem was that everything I was learning from reformers and educators on the ground was flying in the face of some core beliefs of mine that I'd thought were unassailable.

My commitment to the idea of protecting workers' rights traces back to my childhood awareness of the progressive movement, when I learned that unions have played a vital role in defending the rights of working people and making sure that everyone in our society has an opportunity to prosper, not just the wealthy and not just heads of corporations. I still believe in that idea.

And yet wherever I would go in the American school system, even back when I was making *The First Year*, I ran into a conflicting idea, which is that teachers' unions have played a big role in perpetuating the problems that plague our schools. When I was filming scenes in schools, as soon as the cameras were turned off, people would quietly tell me, "You know, we just can't fix these things until we change the unions," or, "The only reason why our school is succeeding is that we don't have a union contract." I was amazed to hear these sentiments from everybody: administrators, principals, school board members, and even teachers.

And so at a certain point in the middle of making the movie, I had to decide whether to bring out this really uncomfortable truth or to back away from it and hedge it. I was worried that maybe I was betraying the ideals I shared with so many friends and family members, and I was afraid people I admire would turn on me. But I started to realize that this kind of thinking keeps things from getting any better and that protecting the status quo so as not to offend anyone does nothing to help kids.

In the end I made a pact with myself that I wasn't going to pull any punches. I would be fair and honest—not sensationalistic—but I was going to speak the truth that reasonable people who were in the trenches were telling me. And it wasn't just about the teachers' unions. I decided to be tough on all of the adults whenever they put their own interests ahead of those of the kids—starting with my own hypocrisy in driving past three public schools with my own children. In the film, I reveal the very uncomfortable truth about the role of the Democratic Party, which receives more campaign contributions from the teachers' unions than from any other source, as well as the parade of politicians who give lip service to education reform but refuse to take the hard steps necessary to make it happen.

I also have to say that the picture of unions and their role in education is not a black-and-white one. I've gotten to know union leaders who I think understand that the reforms we need will mean some serious adjustments on the part of their members, and that we need to rethink the rigid systems we've gotten locked into since the New Deal era. At the same time, these progressive union leaders can't get too far ahead of their members. And they understandably don't want to give aid and comfort to some politicians who are in fact antiworker and are at least as interested in undermining the power of labor as they are in improving our schools.

So these union leaders are walking a political tightrope. I hope that more and more of them will find the courage to do the right things in support of true reform and that they'll be able to bring the vast majority of union members along with them.

As far as the film is concerned, I hope the fairness and honesty I've tried to bring to this issue will be obvious to audiences, and I hope people will try to take what I'm offering and use it to help illuminate ways to improve our schools for the benefit of kids, rather than to bash teachers or unions or anyone else. But in the end that depends on the goodwill of people I have no control over. All I can do is try to describe the situation as I see it as truthfully as possible, and that's what I've tried to do in *Waiting for "Superman."*

Despite all the dysfunction and controversy reflected in *Waiting for "Superman,"* I hope the overriding impression that people take away from the movie is a hopeful one. I didn't want to make a second film about education unless I could direct it in such a way that it would have a powerful impact and hold out some promise that it is possible to fix our schools.

In the ten years since I made *The First Year* and experienced my own "first year" immersion in five tough urban schools, I've witnessed the emergence of a new generation of educators who are doing amazing things and have given me new hope for the future of our schools. Toward the end of *Waiting for "Superman,"* I tell the story of test pilot Chuck Yeager's attempt to break the sound barrier, despite the skeptics who considered it impossible. Yeager did it, and his accomplishment was not just about proving or disproving a scientific theory. It was far more profound and important because it shattered people's perceptions of what was possible. I believe we're now experiencing that same kind of breakthrough of belief on education reform.

Ten years ago, I would hear even the most ambitious and idealistic educators say it was impossible to get great results in tough neighborhoods. Dedicated teachers would say, "I make great strides with the kids during the day, but after a night at home, with all the social problems that plague poor families, the progress has been wiped out." But that's not what happens at such schools as the KIPP schools and Harlem Children's Zone (HCZ), which serve families that have similar problems. And so I believe it's no exaggeration to compare educators such as David Levin, Mike Feinberg, and Geoffrey Canada to an American hero such as Chuck Yeager.

Many members of this new generation are products of Teach For America who are not just infused with the idealism of the New Frontier/Peace Corps mentality but also bring with them a powerful sort of pragmatism, a toughness that says things like "No Excuses" (the KIPP schools) and "Whatever It Takes" (HCZ).

In the film, the breaking-the-sound-barrier sequence is meant to address the most stubborn of the darker voices in people's heads—the naysaying voices that not only deny the possibility of meaningful change but also carry a subtle bigotry about what poor kids can—or cannot—accomplish. Showing Yeager's X-1 blasting through the stratosphere and hearing the amazing statistics of success achieved by those great educators, I hope to shatter another kind of barrier, still present and dangerously invisible—the stubborn belief that "Those kids can't learn."

How tragic would it be if no one in America knew about these incredible breakthroughs? What if it could be done—but no one knew it?

Do I like to dream about *Waiting for "Superman"* becoming a catalyst for fixing our nation's schools? Of course. But I'm also very aware that I'm "just a filmmaker" and that there are severe limits to the impact I can have on the public debate. I'm very mindful of how quickly attitudes can change and that a movie, no matter how successful, will usually have only a limited effect.

But I'm still optimistic—not because of my movie, but because of the people I've gotten to meet who are working on the front lines of the battle for reform—people who, as Geoffrey Canada says, "are doing it every day." I've seen amazing teachers fighting against all odds, incredible schools shining brightly in very tough neighborhoods, and determined parents who are demanding great educations for their kids.

And so, a year from today, after the movie has been widely seen, what do I hope the reaction will be when I say, "I made a film about public education"? Will I still get a polite stare, or an empty compliment like, "That's so noble"? Maybe. But I hope viewers of *Waiting for "Superman"* will have a very different feeling when they drive past their neighborhood school—a feeling that something very profound has changed—something that can't be counted or measured: the emergence of the belief that *it's possible.*

The Road to Super Tuesday

Lesley Chilcott

Producer Lesley Chilcott has collaborated with director Davis Guggenheim on the 2006 Academy Award–winning documentary *An Inconvenient Truth*, the documentary feature *It Might Get Loud* (2009), the Barack Obama biographical film for the Democratic National Convention, *A Mother's Promise* (2008), and *Waiting for "Superman"* (2010), on which she also served as the second unit director.

Chilcott's other credits include a feature documentary about cartoonist Gahan Wilson, *Gahan Wilson: Born Dead, Still Weird* (2007), and the short films *It Was a Dark and Silly Night* (2007) and *Ed I Hide* (2006).

Chilcott worked at MTV Networks on large multicamera shows, including the creation of the first MTV Movie Awards as well as other specials and shows. After MTV, Chilcott moved on to produce music videos and commercials as an independent producer, working with numerous distinguished directors and advertising agencies, producing hundreds of commercials and public service announcements over the past fifteen years.

In 2008, Chilcott cofounded the nonprofit Unscrew America, which continues her dedication to sustainability and environmental issues. She is also a green correspondent for several magazines.

I'm not a parent, and yet I've felt like one ever since I started making *Waiting for "Superman."* Until now, I don't think I've read sixteen books on any single subject *ever*, to say nothing of hundreds of scholarly studies, research reports, articles, interviews, speeches, and blog postings. Practically everyone who has attended school has an opinion about what is right and (more important) what is wrong with our educational system.

But no matter how many reports you read or statistics you study, they all fade into the background once you begin spending time with families who are wrestling with the real-world problems that underlie all the arguments—in many cases, families desperately doing everything they can to get their child into the one good school in their neighborhood.

We filmed many families over the course of many months, and after a short time the kids whose stories we tell in the film became, in effect, "our kids." I woke up with them and, with our cameras rolling, saw them go through their morning routines— Emily brushing her teeth, Francisco tucking in his oversize white shirt, and Daisy stuffing her notebooks into the extra-large backpack she managed to hoist and carry. The same routine happens every morning in every neighborhood in every city and, like "our kids," not enough kids are heading off to great schools.

Cool Teachers

If, ten years ago, you had asked me what was wrong with our public education system, I would have answered, "lack of money." Having grown up in California hearing all about Proposition 13, the famous constitutional amendment enacted in 1978 that drastically limited property taxes and therefore local funding of schools, I had the impression that the diversion of public funds away from schools was the reason our education system had suffered. Later, when I moved to Arizona, and Colorado after that, I heard the same stories about cuts to school programs, driven by tax reductions. As a young student myself, I had no context for these stories, but I could see how the cuts affected me when some of my favorite classes—classes that combined fun with real learning—were taken away.

Lack of money has had, and continues to have, an impact on the quality of schooling in many parts of our country, and it exacerbates inequalities that already exist. But as I've learned more about the problem, I've discovered that there are other factors that are more important—including one I couldn't help noticing even as a kid.

Moving from one school to another enabled me to experience a lot of different teachers. Some were amazing, each in his or her unique style, and I remember them to this day. There was the sly Mr. Quass, who made science experiments feel like the solutions to intriguing mysteries; Mr. Kettelhut, in his itchy formal jackets, treating the study of grammar like a challenging and enjoyable game; and Mrs. Beta, whose very long eye-blinks somehow allowed her to explain to us that a book was not merely a story, but a puzzle that could be read on many levels. It was the good teachers, more than the facilities or a great gym or classroom size, that stood out at every school I went to.

Why does almost everyone seem to have a story about how one special teacher got through to them, changed them, and reshaped their life forever? Could it be that teaching is just about the most important job in the world? And could it be that, in the end, the challenge of fixing America's schools comes down to putting great teachers into classrooms and giving them the tools they need to do what they do best?

We need to appreciate and value great teaching more in America. I spent a brief period of my life in Japan teaching English classes to businessmen and -women at large corporations. I also tutored private students preparing for extended trips to the United States and taught an after-school English class to teens once a week. I was very young at the time, and yet I received incredible respect from my students, not because I was such a spectacular teacher, but because *sensei* (teacher) is a title that carries enormous stature in Japanese society.

Japan isn't the only country where the role of teacher is held in high regard. In Finland, teaching is one of the top career choices for graduates, with teaching positions highly coveted. Only one in ten applicants is selected, and teachers tend to come from the very top of their class (unlike in the United States, where they generally come from the bottom 30 percent—with many exceptions, of course). Those who later choose to move on to different careers find that a background in teaching opens doors in almost every corner of Finnish society.

In some parts of the world, teaching is *cool*. Sadly, this is generally not true here in the United States. Our brightest students from our top universities don't generally opt for teaching; instead, they flock to jobs on Wall Street or at management consulting firms. (Judging by recent economic developments, this has not been working out so well—for those graduates or for the country as a whole.)

It's time for a major cultural shift if we hope to really improve the American educational system. We need to dramatically increase the profession's cool factor. Teaching should be considered one of the most important jobs you can have—which of course it is. (Think about it: If we want to effectively tackle such challenges as global warming, poverty, or health care—any issue really—we must have educated engineers, scientists, economists, legislators, managers, and an educated citizenry to oversee and guide them. Education is ground zero for solving society's problems.) And we need to rethink how we recruit, train, evaluate, and reward great teachers so that the highest possible standards are created and maintained.

As Michelle Rhee, chancellor of the District of Columbia school system, says in a speech excerpted in our film, "I believe that that mind-set has to be completely flipped on its head. Unless you can show that you are bringing positive results for kids, then you cannot have the *privilege* of teaching in our schools and teaching our children."

I love the way Rhee says that: Teaching should be a *privilege*, an honor undertaken with the highest ambition in mind—to groom, educate, and inspire the next generation.

I'm not sure how we've missed this simple truth. If, as John F. Kennedy put it, "children are the world's most valuable resource and its best hope for the future," why are we letting the adults screw things up for them?

When I began producing *Waiting for "Superman,"* the one thing I knew about education—or should have known from my own experience—was the most basic truth: that great teachers are the key. Research shows, in fact, that the single most important factor in improving student achievement is great teaching. But I was distracted by all the competing noise and theory I'd heard and the books and blogs I was now digesting morning and night, trying to come up with a way to cut through all the rhetoric and get to the bottom line: millions and millions of kids are not getting the education they need, and deserve. Maybe, just maybe, there was a way to break it all down into its essential elements, and highlight the solutions that are already out there and working. Yet director Davis Guggenheim and I weren't sure if this could really be done. (Davis and I had formed a documentary company after *An Inconvenient Truth*, the first documentary I produced, which told two stories: former vice president Al Gore's lifelong crusade against global warming, as well as a comprehensive breakdown of exactly what global warming was.) It seemed almost impossible.

My Learning Curve

Not having studied the issues surrounding education before developing *Waiting for "Superman,"* I wasn't sure of the best way to get a crash course in this complicated, multilayered subject. Previously, when I produced *An Inconvenient Truth,* I had a head start, having been worried about our impact as humans on the environment since third grade, when I'd sent away for my conservation sticker kit. I was eight years old and obsessed with performing all the tasks the kit described for boosting efficiency around the house so I could earn the reward of putting the little energy-saver stickers on each window. (It never occurred to me that I could just apply the stickers without actually performing any of the tasks to conserve. . . . I delighted in doing all the little steps.)

Over the years, I maintained my interest in energy conservation, environmental degradation, and sustainable management of the planet's resources. Twenty-five years later, our problems in these areas had grown bigger than ever. Our gluttonous consumption of fossil fuels, inefficient farming practices, and failure to develop renewable sources of energy had brought us to the brink of an economic, social, and moral crisis. So when I met Al Gore and watched his amazing slide show, I was ready to use my filmmaking skills to help him educate the masses about this issue. Thanks to the talents of a great team of professionals, the global success of *An Inconvenient Truth* was the gratifying result.

But the issues surrounding the American public education system were another matter for me. Other than my brief stint at teaching in Japan, I had little personal background in education: I'd majored in business and, before getting into the entertainment business, had wanted to start a vegetarian fast-food chain. Like most people, I knew that as a country, we were becoming less competitive economically and that our test scores were declining. But how did it all break down? And what could I, as a filmmaker, contribute to the national debate on the issue and the attempt to move the needle on school reform?

As I began to study the problem, the answers started to emerge—in the form of unmistakable patterns that appeared in many of the books, countless articles, and studies I read and stories I encountered. And when we began to interview experts, journalists, authors, and successful reformers, the same patterns appeared. This was not unique to me. Davis, as well as the rest of our creative team, and our researchers were noticing the same patterns as well.

One of these patterns was the appearance of the same hopeful pockets of success—reformers with schools around the country that have beaten the odds and managed to produce consistently excellent results, even with, or especially with, students whom mainstream educators label "at-risk." The more we looked, the more we kept encountering the same names and stories. We soon realized that our movie had to show some of these pioneering schools—schools that worked—to as many people as possible.

We also noticed that, varied and unique as these successful schools were, they also seemed to have at least one thing in common: pragmatism. In these schools, ideology isn't allowed to get in the way of meeting children's needs. If a student is behind in reading, he is tutored until he catches up. If a class tests poorly on a particular subject, the teacher reevaluates and adjusts the lesson plan and tackles the topic again until the kids get it. If a few kids are drifting away during class rather than paying attention, the teacher notices and experiments with new approaches until a way is found to engage every last student. And if a teacher is not doing a consistently good job, coaching, advice, or training is provided—and if that doesn't work, the teacher is out. It's not about union or non-union, nor is it about any particular educational philosophy, theory, or system. It's about setting high expectations and creating accountability for teachers as well as students. The only thing that matters are results for kids. Davis and I discovered this pragmatic, no-excuses attitude repeated over and over again in effective schools.

Another pattern involved deeply ingrained social attitudes. Back when I was teaching in Japan, I heard a story that illustrates the difference between kindergarten kids in Japan and their peers in America—as well as the difference in their schools.

Picture a teacher with a group of kindergarteners gathered in a circle around her. "Today," she says, "we're going to learn to draw a picture of Daddy." In the American classroom, each child is given a piece of paper and a bunch of crayons and told to draw his or her own daddy. The teacher walks from table to table, offering help, advice, and praise for those twenty-five separate, different pictures.

In the Japanese classroom, the approach is very different. The teacher has an easel, and the children gather around her to talk about what Daddy looks like. One child says, "He is medium height." Another says, "He wears a suit." A third says, "He has dark hair." Together they draw a group image of Daddy, which represents the combined efforts of all the children.

This story elicits interesting reactions from people. Some may point out that the idea of a "group image" wouldn't work very well in our heterogeneous society. In Japan, almost every dad has dark hair, and many wear suits to work. You don't have that kind of homogeneity in the United States. Others say, "America is all about individualism and we emphasize our differences. Every kid draws his or her own picture because we are all different and unique. That's how we unlock the creativity inside each child."

But the more I've thought about this difference of approach, the more I've realized looking at this story as stamping out individuality and creativity misses the point. Rather than suppressing the individual through group-think, the Japanese drawing of Daddy symbolizes the fact that all the kids in the class are learning together, with no one left out. This approach is reflected in most facets of Japanese schooling where all kids can learn, and more important, do learn, and this includes scoring well on tests.

By contrast, in the American classroom, some kids do well while many fall behind. The class moves on to the next grade level as individuals, not as a group, and only the students who perform exceptionally well get extra attention. The others often fall through the cracks. And maybe this is deemed okay by some people; since we're all individuals, we have come to think that not everyone can always succeed.

Japan's educational system is not perfect, and its international scores have been declining in recent years. Even so, among the thirty developed countries, Japanese students rank number 3 in science and number 6 in math, compared to number 21 in science and number 25 in math—the scores of American students. Now, I'm a filmmaker who didn't study statistics in school, but I'm thinking this doesn't bode well for our future either as a group or as individuals.

There is irony in that we encourage creativity in our kids here in the United States and yet we don't encourage creativity in how we run our schools. This is another reason why we are not producing results. And yet it is a defining characteristic in the high-performing schools we discovered while making the film.

As a nation, we've tried to take steps to change the "every child for herself" philosophy of American education. We even passed a famous bipartisan reform, an effort to include everyone in the group, under the title of No Child Left Behind. But that title remains more an empty promise than a reality—at least, in the mainstream schools we visited and learned about. In the exceptional schools where new ways of pursuing excellence are being developed, there is a real effort to help *every* child achieve his potential. All kids can, and must, learn. It's another pattern we noticed and tried to capture in *Waiting for "Superman."*

The importance of freedom as a precursor to reform is what has created so much excitement around charter schools—schools that enjoy public financial support but that operate outside the controls that hamper traditional public school systems.

In *Waiting for "Superman,"* we celebrate the successes of the high-performing charter schools—the KIPP Schools, Harlem Success Academy, Harlem Children's Zone, the SEED schools, and Summit Prep, among others.

On the other hand, a June 2009 study by the Center for Research on Education Outcomes (CREDO) at Stanford University showed that only 17 percent of charter schools—just under one in five—are producing results that are significantly better than comparable public schools.[1] This is important. It reminds us that the charter school label is not a magic bullet that guarantees excellent education all by itself. Nor are charter schools the only answer. We should support all good public schools, whatever their form, regular public, charter or magnet—whatever works. Back to pragmatism.

And pragmatism is certainly the approach practically every parent and student takes. The families we ended up following when we filmed *Waiting for "Superman"* probably couldn't give you a dictionary definition of a charter school, but parents like Nakia, whose daughter Bianca appears in the film, know that in their neighborhood, the really good public schools, such as Harlem Success Academy (HSA) and Harlem Children's Zone, just happen to be charters. Nakia applied to HSA not because it was a charter, but because it's a great school, with effective leadership and phenomenal teachers. And in HSA's case, that translates to 100 percent of third graders passing the math exam and 95 percent of third graders passing English. This isn't just good, it's extraordinary.

An incredible exception, difficult to duplicate . . . right? Maybe not. Seven blocks away, Harlem Children's Zone has posted similar results. At the Zone's Promise Academy II, 100 percent of the third graders scored at or above grade level in the statewide math exams, and 100 percent of the Promise Academy I third graders were at or above grade level in math.

Hmm, let's see . . . 100 percent proficiency. Two different sets of schools. It's hard to argue with reform that boosts the learning of not some, not many, but *all* students.

A New Kind of Lottery

One Monday morning while we were deeply immersed in rearranging colored index cards containing various story ideas on the wall in our edit bay, Davis came into the production office with an amazing idea. He'd just read an op-ed piece by *New York Times* columnist Thomas Friedman about a local SEED school and the lottery it used to select students for the coming year. The SEED schools are the only urban public boarding schools in the country, designed to provide underserved kids with a round-the-clock nurturing atmosphere. Free from distractions that might exist at home, SEED students live on campus starting in the sixth grade and learn life skills in addition to academic ones.

At the time of the article Davis read, the original SEED school in Washington, D.C., was doing so well that another was opening in Baltimore, and the lottery Friedman attended selected the students for this new school. As Friedman put it, this was "no ordinary lottery. The winners didn't win cash, but a ticket to a better life." Davis thought it could be the story that could tie everything together.

The idea came at the perfect moment for us all as filmmakers. Up to this point, we had a working framework for the range of issues we wanted to cover in the movie. But something was missing—a group of deeply personal stories that everyone could relate to and that would show the very real consequences of our flailing education system.

The lottery, we realized, was the story that would tie everything together as a whole. Talk about ironic—a collection of separate but wonderful schools all around the country has figured out what really works in education. But there aren't enough schools like these or enough spaces for kids to attend. So instead we hold lotteries to decide which kids will be lucky enough to get a decent education. This year in New York City alone, over 40,000 kids who applied to charter schools didn't get in. There were so many lotteries last year when we were filming, in fact, that the papers started calling the day on which many of the lotteries were held Super Tuesday, just like an election— unfortunately, complete with politics. I could not get over this reference to Super Tuesday, and it stuck with me. The moniker seemed like a casual approach, in name, to a profoundly serious problem. It shows, once again, that it's completely unfair that there are not enough spaces for these kids and a clear indictment of how dysfunctional our system has become.

I often joke with friends, "Why is it that I have a choice of seven different kinds of peanut butter, not even counting the organic brands, and yet kids in my neighborhood don't even have the choice of a single great public school?" If America is the land of choice, where are the choices for getting a great education? Instead of choice, we have lotteries.

So our team began a nationwide hunt for different types of school lotteries and for a group of families who were desperately trying to get into one of the few good schools available to them. We attended parent information sessions and talked to families as they were applying for slots at highly ranked local schools. We recruited admission directors to help us locate kids whose stories we might tell, and we visited school information fairs and chatted with the parents we encountered there. It's a big step for a family to allow a team of filmmakers to follow them around for several months. The five families who appear in *Waiting for "Superman"*—as well as others who didn't end up in the finished film—were extraordinarily brave to let us into their lives. All of them wanted something better for their kids, and I think they hoped that, by allowing us into their lives, they could help shine a light on the fact that *all* parents want a good education for their kids . . . and they *all* deserve it.

In the end, after shooting footage at schools in Texas, New Orleans, Brooklyn, Pittsburgh, and North Carolina, we had to make some tough choices, limited both by time and budgetary considerations. The communities highlighted in *Waiting for "Superman"* are in Northern California, East Los Angeles, New York City, and Washington, D.C. But of course the challenges, opportunities, and heartbreaks they represent are replicated in thousands of neighborhoods in all fifty states.

All of us on the filmmaking team quickly became immersed in the lives of our five exemplary families and their long march toward the fateful lotteries, which are generally held in the late spring. We put their pictures up on our wall in the edit bay. As we watched them, they watched us. We knew we had a responsibility to them to get their stories right.

I became very attached to all "our kids." Bianca was only in kindergarten, yet here she was, reading a million miles a minute and narrating her life for us, on camera and unprompted, overly wise for her six years.

Francisco was bright and curious, and could clearly read well, as we saw every time we filmed at his house, yet in school he struggled with reading—we found ourselves wondering and worrying about the disconnect.

Fifth grader Anthony had the wisdom to tell Davis that what he wanted was to find a good school to attend—and was already talking about the importance of education for his own kids, someday in the faraway future.

Daisy was good at a variety of subjects and talked in clear, graceful English about becoming a doctor, a vet, or a surgeon—yet she was stuck in an English language learner class intended for kids with problems with fluency.

And Emily, the ideal student from a "nice," middle-class family with all the advantages, loved studying and relished math camp—but just didn't test well and needed extra help.

Our decision to include Emily in the film was an important one. Most Americans agree that our education system is in crisis, and most realize that the problem is worst in our underserved communities—less affluent, often located in the inner city, disproportionately populated by minority-group members. But the dirty little secret uncovered in our film (and elsewhere) is that our middle- and upper-class communities are suffering as well. When we talk about U.S. students ranking twenty-fifth in math, we're not just talking about underserved communities, we're talking *overall*.

This is about all kids in all neighborhoods. The middle-class school campus might be well-groomed, offer great athletics, and provide other attractive features. But when you look behind the superficial structure at many such schools and examine the actual data on student performance, you often find that the top-performing kids are *dragging up* the overall test scores, masking the mediocrity in which the *bottom 75 percent* are stuck. And the bottom 75 percent of students in American high schools amounts to about 11 million people. That's a very big number.

This is one major reason why we're not producing large numbers of scientists and doctors in this country anymore; the majority are coming from other countries. This means we are not only less educated, but also less economically competitive—a problem that could have ramifications for decades.

I remember each of the lotteries as if it just happened last week. We ran four cameras at each lottery so we could follow not only our kids and their families but others as well. Of course, we had absolutely no idea what was going to happen, and I struggled to listen to the names of "winning" students being called, watching our kids and their families as they grappled with this emotional and somewhat absurd event, and making sure all our cameras were in the right places, while at the same time feeling a knot in my stomach.

Often the tension was almost too much to bear. At one lottery, I wanted to throw the bingo ball cage across the room—it didn't look to me as if there were enough balls in the cage for each grade. There were simply not enough spaces.

Another time, I watched a lottery official reach into a bin of folded index cards inscribed with individual names in Sharpie pen and accidentally grab two, only to shake one off and give a classroom seat to the student whose card was left in his hand. Whose card did he drop? Was it one of our kids? Did one of our kids just lose his or her chance at a good education?

The lotteries with computer-generated numbers were no better. Maybe the numbers were larger and the process more technologically advanced than a hand reaching into a bin or basket, but the results were just as arbitrary.

Adding to the tension was the fact that, like sports fans agonizing over a playoff game, we became ridiculously superstitious.

I won't reveal here what happened at the lotteries, but let's just say that we alternated between crossing our fingers and thinking our cameras could be a talisman for luck, impossible as it was, and thinking we might be a curse, because no matter where we went in the end, not enough kids got in—not even close. The ball bounced the wrong way more often than not. Of course, we knew deep down it wasn't us either way, it was just the odds. But the odds sucked. And there we were, witnessing heartbreak after heartbreak. The only consolation was the hope that if we shared these horror stories—and they were horror stories—that we might be able to help bring about change.

When I interviewed the parents afterward, no matter how professional I aimed to be, I couldn't keep the tears from forming. I know that many of our camera people shot through bleary eyes. And yet we knew we had to be there. The absurdity of our education crisis had to be seen in a new and immediate way. All the damning statistics don't really resonate until you look at one kid, one parent, and one bingo ball.

There is no reason for this kind of mess in 2010. As journalist Jonathan Alter says in the film, the educational reform battle has reached a new stage, for one simple reason: "We now know what works." Political dogma and customary ways of thinking must be set aside to provide what's best for our kids.

There is no more waiting for *"Superman."* There is only you and me.

PART II

FRANCISCO

INTRODUCTION

Francisco's Story

Francisco is a first grader in the Bronx, New York. He goes to an overcrowded public school where it's easy to slip through the cracks. Maria, Francisco's mother, knows the challenges Francisco faces, because she graduated from Bronx public schools herself.

Maria was the first in her family to go to college. She has a graduate degree and is a social worker. As a parent, she's done everything she can to give her son opportunities that the local schools can't provide. She has enrolled him in two after-school reading programs at a local city college, she studies with him every night, and she's reaching out to his teacher for more help. But Francisco's teacher is overworked with too many students, and Maria keeps being stymied by "the system."

As *Waiting for "Superman"* begins, Maria is running out of options. She has applied Francisco to seven charter schools that all offer excellent academic programs, but he's been denied admission every time. Maria is now forced to look for schools outside of the Bronx. She has applied on Francisco's behalf to the Harlem Success Academy, a rigorous charter school that offers the individualized help Francisco needs as an English language learner. Harlem Success Academy is a forty-five-minute commute from their apartment and it's Francisco's last chance to get into a good school. If Francisco doesn't get in, he will have to stay at his overcrowded school and risk falling behind.

Francisco is one of 792 applicants applying for 40 spots. He has a 5 percent chance of getting in. . . .

How Schools Kill Neighborhoods— and Can Help Save Them

Bill Strickland

Bill Strickland was born in 1947 and grew up in Manchester, an inner-city neighborhood of Pittsburgh. His life changed when he became inspired by high school art teacher Frank Ross, a skilled artisan on the potter's wheel. The relationship that Ross and Strickland initiated with a revolving mound of clay gave form to the future vision of Manchester Craftsmen's Guild (MCG). The Guild began as an after-school arts program in a donated North Side rowhouse that Strickland secured while still a college student at the University of Pittsburgh. In 1969, he graduated cum laude with a bachelor's degree in American history and foreign relations.

Due to Strickland's successful track record with MCG, he was asked in 1971 to assume leadership of Bidwell Training Center, which was addressing the problem of widespread unemployment caused by the decline of the steel industry through vocational training to displaced and underemployed workers. Strickland's involvement in both MCG and BTC doubled the strength of Manchester Bidwell Corporation's ability to help the community. Strickland envisioned a template for social change and began to form relationships with businesses, government officials, and individuals who shared his vision.

Today, Manchester Bidwell Corporation has evolved into a national model for education, culture, and hope. MCG Youth & Arts and MCG Jazz are both programs of Manchester Craftsmen's Guild, which serves around 3,900 young people each year. MCG Youth offers classes and workshops in ceramics, photography, digital imaging, and design art. MCG Arts gives students a chance to work intensively with visiting artists of national and international stature through exhibitions, lectures, workshops, residencies, and school visits. MCG Jazz is dedicated to preserving, promoting, and presenting jazz music by bringing audiences together with jazz artists at its 350-seat music hall in Pittsburgh for innovative four-day performances and recordings. Bidwell Training Center provides market-driven career education created through strong partnerships with leading local industries. The center offers accredited associate's degree and diploma programs in fields as varied as culinary arts, chemical laboratory technologies, health careers, horticulture, and office technology.

The model provided by Manchester Bidwell Corporation works so well that Bill Strickland is working on replicating it throughout the country. Strickland and his family reside on the north side of Pittsburgh.

———————

Having spent the first sixty-three years of life within the same six-block city neighborhood in Pittsburgh, Pennsylvania, I have watched the growth, decline, and—hopefully—the rebirth of our city's school system and in particular the schools near and in my neighborhood. From elementary school through high school, I attended public schools and lived through experiences that, as an adult, I have come to understand were not unique to me. In these pages, I hope to articulate some of the insights I developed as a result.

The elementary school I attended served children from a variety of ethnic backgrounds, including German, Slovak, Italian, Greek, Polish, Russian, and African-American. It was not uncommon to hear many languages echoing in the school hallways and spoken in the neighborhood. In this and many other ways, the school and the neighborhood were closely intertwined. Civic functions, sports activities, the parent-teacher association, and many church events were staged in the elementary school, which was at the center of community life. Thankfully, the school was not dysfunctional or locked down for security reasons as many are today. If it had been, these events and other opportunities for binding the community together through our shared educational space simply would not have occurred.

Life experience has since taught me that the special role of the school in community life is—or should be—a common feature almost everywhere. Parents, particularly mothers, follow the life experiences of their children, good or bad. This phenomenon is well recognized by the headmasters and boards of private schools throughout America, which deliberately promote themselves as members of the community and work hard to make sure that communication between the schools and their families is frequent, of high quality, and sustained. Unfortunately, not all public schools are gifted with leaders who recognize the importance of the school-community bond. As a result, similar opportunities for community and parental involvement are never realized. In time, the school becomes a lonely citadel, isolated, shut off, and afraid, rather than a hopeful, interactive, engaged member of its community.

This troubles me greatly. I am an unabashed advocate for public education. One reason—a very personal one—is that my own life as a young adult was dramatically altered for the better by an arts teacher, Frank Ross, who believed in the redemptive power of the arts and exemplified that power in his role as public school teacher and mentor to countless young people like me. Mr. Ross created within his classroom a spirit of learning and adventure, in which education became fun and from which the marvels and opportunities of the wide world were accessible. Thanks to him, I became an educator myself. Today I run the Manchester Bidwell Corporation (MBC), a nonprofit center/ school that trains at-risk adults for market-specific careers in industry as well as using the arts as a motivational strategy to recover at-risk public schoolchildren. Now I'm able to do for many of today's youngsters what Mr. Ross did for me. So I know the amazing power that education can have to transform lives, and I'm committed to making that power available to as many young people as possible.

Unfortunately, in too many communities, schools like the one I attended and teachers like Mr. Ross are not available. The results are distressing and very costly. When students do not achieve in school, they often lose interest, fail to graduate, and become liabilities rather than assets to the communities where they live. When the number of failed students exceeds the number of successful graduates in a community, the culture becomes one of failure rather than one of success, leading to a downward spiral for the entire community. Large numbers of people without jobs place an enormous strain on community resources through domestic violence, drug abuse, vandalism, and theft. Crime goes up, property values plummet, businesses leave, the tax base erodes, and the local infrastructure begins to crumble. Such communities are often designated as high-risk investment zones, so financial institutions begin to refuse to write mortgages or make business loans. Over time, what may once have been a prosperous community becomes a ghetto, a place with no hope and no prospects for the future.

Of course, the downward spiral affects the schools as well. Lacking financial resources and filled with students from dysfunctional families, the schools struggle to fulfill their educational mission. The culture of failure becomes more and more self-reinforcing. The school, in a sense, is a weather vane for the community, reflecting the good or bad trends that are changing the neighborhood. But it also multiplies the impact of those trends. When many schools are performing badly, the resulting problems can envelop an entire city, county, or region. This situation feeds on itself, and the truth of the old adage "success breeds success and failure breeds failure" becomes very evident.

Educational failure has huge economic costs. Over a lifetime, a high school dropout can expect to earn hundreds of thousands of dollars less than his counterpart who is equipped with a diploma. The money that dropouts fail to earn is not deployed in the community in the form of consumer spending, mortgage payments, or tax revenues. At the same time, dropouts tend to place greater economic strain on public programs by requiring subsidized housing, more uninsured visits to medical facilities, costly drug and alcohol rehabilitation programs, and other social services provided to the unproductive. When these individuals begin numbering in the tens of thousands, the expense is calculated in the tens of millions of dollars.

By contrast, the vast majority of the hundreds of students we work with each year at MBC go on to such colleges as Rhode Island School of Design, the University of Pittsburgh, Rochester Institute of Technology, and even Harvard, as well as to successful employment with companies such as Alcoa, Bayer, Calgon Carbon, Marriott, and UPMC Health System. They end up buying homes, paying taxes, boosting the economy through consumer spending, and creating stable home environments that help their children write success stories of their own. Living examples of success, they stimulate a positive upward spiral in their communities.

The equation is quite clear: Failed schools equal failed communities; successful schools equal thriving communities!

But when we accept this crucial reality, we've only begun the conversation. The next important question is, what kind of school has the best chance of success and the greatest potential for contributing positively to the life of the community? I think the story of MBC offers some clues to the answer.

Our center is located four blocks from my old high school in the North Shore neighborhood of Pittsburgh. Designed by Tasso Katselas, a leading local architect who was a student of Frank Lloyd Wright, it's a handsome structure of adobe-colored brick adorned with skylights, interior arches, and integrated works of art. The physical beauty of the building isn't just a nicety. It's a testimony to the power of good design and a beautiful environment to influence behavior. In our twenty-five-year history, we have had no fights, no drugs, no alcohol, and no thefts of equipment or property. (By contrast, my old high school in the same neighborhood has bars on the windows, steel doors, metal detectors, and security cameras, and is often in lockdown status to dampen the ever-present possibility of violence.)

The MBC center is so appealing that it attracts a wide range of community events, from gourmet food evenings and Chefs Association meetings to sold-out jazz concerts starring world-class artists such as Herbie Hancock and Nancy Wilson. The facilities have been used for ceramic art symposiums, medical association gatherings, and horticultural events that have filled the center with orchids, daffodils, and roses. So powerful a magnet has the center become that graduate students in education and social policy have written case studies about it. In short, our school functions as a center of life and vitality for the community and the entire region.

In schools that matter, the details are critical. The way in which the physical plant is constructed and maintained, the amenities that show caring and thoughtful planning, the foods provided in the cafeteria, the maintenance program that ensures a safe, comfortable, and efficient physical environment, computer and audio-visual equipment that functions well—these and other details must reflect the very best that the school is capable of providing in order to ensure maximum return in the form of student achievement.

This is a lesson that has been forgotten by the leaders of too many public system systems. We've all seen schools that resemble prisons or fortresses. Of course, it's difficult to convince highly skilled administrators and faculty to spend their working lives in such inferior, depressing facilities. Even worse, when we tolerate conditions like these, we send the psychological message that the young people who attend these schools are not worthy of serious investment. No wonder student achievement suffers.

Little things matter! In good schools, great attention is paid to the smallest detail, including things as mundane as replacing a broken computer or fixing a splintered desk in a classroom. Such details, taken together, add up to a big problem if left unattended over time. The mood and atmosphere of the school set the stage for success or failure.

This is especially true with children who come from horrendous social circumstances, such as broken and dysfunctional families. Children who routinely experience violence, drug abuse, hunger, physical deprivation, poor housing, and the absence of positive role models begin their school careers with two strikes against them. If the school simply reflects an already depressed environment, it becomes part of the problem rather than part of the solution.

We simply can't afford to let this happen. A neighborhood school controls substantial resources—money and jobs—as well as being an enormous, very visible, physical presence in the community. It often is *the* primary economic and social factor in a neighborhood. We have to do whatever is necessary to make sure its impact on the community is positive rather than negative.

Of course, achieving this goal requires more than creating an attractive and efficient physical environment (important as that is). It also demands an education system designed for maximum accomplishment.

Creating and maintaining such a system begins at the top, with the school's leader. A good CEO, superintendent, principal, or headmaster is the key component to creating an excellence-based educational culture. This means that a smart selection process must be put in place to identify the appropriate type of person for the job. An education degree may be a useful element in the background of such a leader, but it's certainly not the only qualification I would consider. Individuals with proven skills in innovation, entrepreneurship, business management, and inspirational leadership should be considered. Candidates could be drawn from industry, universities, community organizations, and the nonprofit sector. This is one of many areas where loosening the stranglehold of traditional bureaucratic, political, and union rules is necessary to bring our schools into the twenty-first century.

Once the right leader is selected, he or she must be given the administrative freedom and independence to make rapid situational decisions as well as the resource base needed to support the key administrative and governance initiatives he or she chooses to pursue. In most businesses, the CEO or executive vice president is trusted to make basic choices on behalf of the organization without having to consult with an unwieldy bureaucracy or follow a set of complicated rules. The result is an organization that can respond nimbly to challenges, as well as one in which lines of authority are clear. If the leader makes a mistake, everyone knows who is responsible. Schools should be run on the same basis. Otherwise, problems give rise to finger-pointing and blame-shifting rather than a simple search for solutions.

Giving both power and responsibility to school administrators and teachers means a real shift in how we think about school management. It impacts union work rules, performance measurements, and hiring and firing practices. Willingness to experiment and to change is required on the part of everyone involved in school leadership—teachers, union leaders, administrators, school board members, active parents, local political leaders, and citizens' groups. Change can be challenging, even painful—but the alternative path leads only to continued failure, which is not an acceptable option.

We also need to become more creative and open-minded when it comes to recruiting faculty. Schools need to consider industry and the business world as important sources of faculty to conduct core courses. The current isolation of public schools and their personnel leads to information deprivation. Most educators are unable to equip their students with the requisite skills for today's fast-paced, technology-driven world because their own knowledge base is severely restricted.

By contrast, at MBC we have become adept at incorporating industry best practices into our core operations. A typical model would be our chemical laboratory technology program, now in its fifteenth year. This program grew out of the need for market-ready, sophisticated chemical laboratory technicians capable of functioning to the standards set by industry-leading chemical companies. A senior production technician on loan from a local chemical company's operating unit met with our team to design industry-specific standards for a laboratory technicians' training program. PPG Industries then loaned our center the first instructor for the program, and with other local chemical companies we jointly developed the standards and entry qualifications for the first students. Finally we solicited funding from other industry leaders, such as the Bayer Corporation, which helped us equip a state-of-the-art lab.

The curriculum was so well articulated that 90 percent of the first class graduated and went straight to work with the region's industry-leading firms. Following the same template, we've now placed hundreds of technicians in the chemical and lab tech world, breaking the poverty cycle and providing these students with lifetime career opportunities.

Another example of a successful partnership model is our pharmacy technician program for unemployed and underemployed adults, created through collaboration with the University of Pittsburgh Medical Center (UPMC). The health system made available to us several instructional staff and access to its computer database and clinical practices manuals. Bidwell staff worked side by side with the UPMC faculty to duplicate an industry-leading pharmaceutical program, and UPMC's human resources experts helped us develop testing and interview techniques to select the students with the highest likelihood of succeeding. The first classes were very successful; we placed 90 percent of the students in the UPMC Health System. We have now developed ten classes of health care professionals, who enjoy productive, useful lives and career opportunities that were unavailable to them before. Inspired in part by this positive experience, UPMC has now developed comparable programs in medical coding and medical billing using much the same methodology and strategy. In fact, the UPMC/MBC program has become a model for other community-based training programs around the country.

The key is to place innovation, creativity, and an entrepreneurial spirit at the heart of the school. In this way, the message is sent loud and clear that the school is open for business.

Unfortunately, most public schools are reluctant to forge links with the business sector. If failing schools were willing to take a critical look at their circumstances and ask for help in re-defining themselves, I believe most if not all industry leaders would respond to the call without hesitation—not just out of philanthropic motivations but from self-interest. Business lead-ers are keenly aware that unless we have a qualified workforce trained to world-class standards, America's ability to lead the world as an economic and industrial power will be compro-mised and the future of our country will be put at risk. The era of schools and educators talking only to themselves must come to an end. No system, no matter how innovative, will survive in the modern world by closing itself off to good ideas from a wide array of sources. The sooner we acknowledge this, the sooner we can solve the problem.

Schools need stronger ties to the community in arenas be-yond business as well—for example, in the cultural, artistic, and creative sectors. Dance companies, museums, theaters, visual arts and crafts centers, literacy groups, orchestras, music schools, and many other cultural institutions can be found within strik-ing distance of public schools in most communities. Yet very few public schools take advantage of these enormous resources. Failed schools fail in part due to their inability or unwillingness to seek help on behalf of their students, while successful schools are constantly looking and reaching out. They know that the tal-ents, ideas, and resources that cultural initiatives can bring to troubled public schools can infuse them with life and attract positive public attention in their direction.

One of the many tragic consequences of failing public schools is that cultural programs and the arts get eliminated or drastically cut back in an effort to save money. As an inner-city public school kid whose life was saved by a good art teacher, I consider this a major mistake. Many children can be reached through the arts where other avenues of education simply do not work. The arts bring cheer, visual stimulation, and excitement by their very nature—all key qualities that failing schools lack.

To address this challenge, MBC has created an active partnership with the Pittsburgh public school system where more than four hundred at-risk children come to our center each week for training in the arts, including ceramics, digital imaging, photography, and graphic design. Many of these children are from the group considered most unlikely to finish high school; many have been identified as "incapable of learning." Yet we've found that nothing could be further from the truth. Despite their difficult backgrounds, these students respond very favorably to our positive, life-affirming environment and our highly motivated, committed art teachers. Many have experienced successes that have helped to turn around their entire lives.

It's time we remove fear and defeat from the vocabulary of the schools in our communities. The ultimate price we pay for a failed school is the loss of hope for present and future generations—a price we simply can't afford to pay any longer. And the alternative is amazingly powerful—a school system that becomes a beacon of hope, energy, enlightenment, and growth for entire neighborhoods, communities, and cities. We are working to make this happen in Pittsburgh, and we're convinced that the methods we're using can be applied around the country.

The Difference Is Great Teachers

Eric Hanushek

Eric Hanushek is the Paul and Jean Hanna Senior Fellow at the Hoover Institution of Stanford University. He has been a leader in the development of economic analysis of educational issues, and his work on efficiency, resource usage, and economic outcomes of schools has frequently entered into the design of both national and international educational policy. His newest book, *Schoolhouses, Courthouses, and Statehouses: Solving the Funding-Achievement Puzzle in America's Public Schools*, coauthored with Alfred A. Lindseth (Princeton, NJ: Princeton University Press, 2009), describes how improved school finance policies can be used to meet our achievement goals.

Hanushek is a member of the National Academy of Education and the International Academy of Education as well as a fellow of the Society of Labor Economists and the American Education Research Association. He was awarded the Fordham Prize for Distinguished Scholarship in 2004. He is currently the chair of the board of directors of the National Board for Education Sciences and previously served as deputy director of the Congressional Budget Office.

Hanushek is a Distinguished Graduate of the U.S. Air Force Academy and completed his PhD in economics at the Massachusetts Institute of Technology.

The United States is built on the idea that all individuals should be free to reach their full potential—the "pursuit of happiness" mentioned in the Declaration of Independence as one of the "unalienable rights" all Americans share. And a natural corollary is that society has the responsibility to provide at least the basic tools individuals need to pursue this goal effectively. While many aspects are involved in accomplishing this goal, our schools clearly have a key role. But it is also clear that the schools have not been doing as much as they could to ensure that all Americans have the knowledge and skills they need to succeed in the twenty-first century. As a result, school reform is a topic on many people's minds today—as it should be.

It is becoming broadly recognized that quality teachers are the key ingredient to a successful school and to improved student achievement. Yet standard policies do not ensure that quality teachers are recruited or retained in the profession. Finding solutions to this problem is particularly important given the rate of expected retirements and, commensurately, the huge numbers of new teachers who must be hired over the next decade. Without some significant changes in the current ineffective system for hiring and training teachers, the hope of systematically improving student outcomes is small.

The Importance of Teacher Quality— Myth Versus Reality

But is teacher quality really a crucial variable in determining the success of students? This belief hasn't always been generally accepted.

In 1966, *Equality of Educational Opportunity*, the most extensive investigation of U.S. schools *ever* undertaken, was published. This monumental report, funded by the Office of Education and authorized under the Civil Rights Act of 1964, was written by James S. Coleman and a team of researchers; hence its usual name, the Coleman Report. Based on a superficial understanding of the Coleman Report, many in the decades since then have argued that schools do not matter and that only families and peers affect the student performance.

There is a grain of truth in this belief: Families and peers do have a very important influence on learning. But this does not detract from the importance of schools and teachers. On the contrary, it raises their value.

Unfortunately, the Coleman Report and many subsequent misinterpretations of it have generally confused *measurability* with true effects. Coleman's study showed that some measurable characteristics of schools and classrooms—for example, whether a teacher held a master's degree or the number of students in a classroom—had no clear statistical effect on student performance. Exaggerated and over-generalized, these findings, probably more than anything else, led to the prevailing view that differences among schools and teachers are not very important when it comes to student achievement.

However, extensive research into educational effectiveness since the 1960s has led to very different policy conclusions. One set of research findings is similar to those of the Coleman Report, and one differs significantly. The overall result is a significantly altered perspective on policy.

First, there are very important differences among teachers—a finding that does not surprise most parents or students, who are well aware that some teachers are simply much more skilled and effective than others. Second, these differences are *not* captured by the most commonly used measurements—qualifications, degrees, years of experience, and the like. This latter finding has important implications that I sketch below.

If we can't identify the best teachers by comparing their credentials, we face an obvious and crucial question: How *do* we define a good teacher? It would be wonderful if we could develop a checklist that could be used, for example, by the human resource department in a school district to guide the selection process and thereby reliably identify teachers who will do well in the classroom. Unfortunately, such a checklist is just what researchers have been unable to provide. Instead, the best way to identify a teacher's effectiveness is to observe her classroom performance and specifically what her students learn.

From this new perspective, a good teacher is one who consistently evokes large gains in student learning, while a poor teacher is one who consistently gets small gains in student learning. In other words, the quality of a teacher is best judged by performance in the classroom as reflected in the gains in learning by the students.

The implications of this insight for the crafting of policies to improve student performance are discussed below. But first it is important to understand the impact of teachers on students, which is even greater than most people realize.

First, the magnitude of the differences among teachers is impressive. Let me provide two different indications of teacher quality, each relying on our performance-based definition of teacher quality. Looking at the range of quality for teachers within a single large urban district, teachers near the top of the quality distribution can get an entire year's worth of additional learning out of their students compared to those near the bottom. That is, in a single academic year, a good teacher will get a gain of one and a half grade-level equivalents, while a bad teacher will get a gain equivalent to just half a year.[1]

Alternatively, if we look at just the variations in performance from differences in teacher quality within a typical school, moving from an average teacher to one at the 85th percentile of teacher quality (that is, a teacher ranked among the top 15 percent of all teachers in quality), we find that the high-ranked teacher's students can be expected to move up more than 8 percentile rankings during the course of a school year. In other words, an average student who got one of these good teachers would move from the middle of the achievement distribution (the 50th percentile) to the 58th percentile.

This is a significant improvement. Extrapolate it over several years in a high-ranked teacher's classroom as compared to a middle-of-the-pack teacher, and you can see that the cumulative effect can be huge. And of course the difference in achievement is likely to be much greater when a high-ranked teacher is compared to a lower-than-average teacher.

With these findings in mind, let's reconsider the popular argument that family background is overwhelmingly important and that schools cannot be expected to make up for bad preparation at home. At times, this argument has led to a counsel of despair: "When a school is filled with poor children, many of whom suffer from broken homes, neglectful parents, and deficits in nutrition and health care, there's little or nothing a school can do to produce high-achieving students."

Again, there is a grain of truth here: There is no doubt that the family is very important in influencing a student's preparation for learning. But family is not destiny. The estimates of teacher performance we've cited suggest that having three to four years of good teachers (85th percentile) in a row would generally overcome the average achievement deficit between low-income kids (those on free or reduced-price lunch) and others. In other words, high-quality teachers can make up for the typical deficits that we see in the preparation of kids from disadvantaged backgrounds.

Unfortunately, the current school system does not ensure any such three- or four-year run of high-quality teachers. In fact, it is currently just as likely that the typical student will get a run of *bad* teachers, with equally large achievement *losses*.

Furthermore, the naturally occurring variation in teacher quality helps to encourage observers to underestimate the importance of teachers for student achievement. If the typical student gets a good teacher one year and a bad teacher the next, the differing effects of these teachers on the student's skill level will tend to cancel out. So when we look at the achievement scores earned by this student and thousands of others in the same situation, we are left with large variations in achievement that tend to track family background. These simple observations might lead to the conclusion that teachers and schools are not very important—when just the opposite is true.

Similarly, when we look at overall achievement levels, such as those reported regularly in the media in the form of "school accountability report cards," we might also be led to believe that all the good teachers are in the suburbs and all the bad teachers are in the core cities. The scores in suburban schools are, after all, almost invariably higher than those in inner-city schools that serve disadvantaged populations. But this observation again simply reflects that families are important. It does not say much about the quality of individual teachers. In fact, detailed analyses of achievement differences in terms of learning gains indicate that the differences among teachers within any given school are generally much larger than the differences across schools. In other words, schools serving disadvantaged students tend to have both very good and very bad teachers—and the same holds true for schools serving more advantaged kids.[2]

It's easy to see how, in practice, this situation can result in misleading statistics. In a school with many poor kids, the students may come to class with learning deficits that are larger than a single teacher can overcome in a year. Thus, even a good teacher who stimulates above-average gains in performance may not be able to bring the typical student all the way up to grade level. In the same way, in a school serving more advantaged students, the typical achievement level might be sufficiently high that even a bad teacher does not drag students down below grade level. This does not mean that all of the teachers in the advantaged school are good; rather, it means that the teachers had good students to work with, thanks to the advantages created by their families or the skills of their previous teachers.

The Economic Implication

It is useful to put these statistics into perspective. As parents and policy makers know, schooling yields high economic rewards: People with more schooling reap the reward of less unemployment, better jobs, and higher incomes.

But the conventional wisdom about the economic value of education ignores the importance of the *quality* of learning students enjoy. The usual comparisons involve different levels of school attainment, such as between high school graduates and dropouts, or between college graduates and those who left school earlier. It is less common to trace the impacts of higher achievement—that is, of learning more in school.

It turns out that knowledge gained through education has a very large payoff. To begin with, students who learn more are more apt to complete high school, to enter college, and to complete a degree. This natural behavior leads to the attainment results that everybody is aware of.

But in addition, increased incomes go to those who know more. If we compare two high school graduates with differing achievement levels, the one with higher achievement tends to earn more. The difference leads to sizable differences over a lifetime as these returns to knowledge accrue year after year.[3]

Modern economies have a voracious appetite for the most skilled people. This demand has led to a widening of the income distribution built simply on what people know. Over time, more-skilled workers have pulled away economically from less-skilled workers—even when both groups have completed the same level of school. An enormous amount of media attention goes to executive salaries and the incomes of the very rich, but the market rewards enjoyed by skilled individuals are much more relevant for most of the population, and these are significant. The student who is happy to coast through school thinking that graduation is all that counts will be brought back to reality when he reaches the labor market.

Still another aspect of student achievement has almost completely escaped notice. If we look around the world, it is clear that countries with high educational achievement also have high rates of economic growth. This relationship is especially important to our future as a nation, because economic growth is what provides us with increasing incomes and greater economic well-being over time. Moreover, the relationship between educational achievement and growth is very strong. Extrapolating from past economic growth, the educational differences between us and, say, the United Kingdom or Germany could amount to *trillions* of dollars in additional gross domestic product (GDP) in the decades to come. The potential impact dwarfs the $1 trillion spent on economic stimulus funding in response to the recession in 2008 and 2009.

Thus, it's extremely disturbing to realize that student achievement in the United States currently ranks below average among the developed countries of the world, as revealed by regular testing of student achievement in math and science across a large number of countries. It is not just the United Kingdom and Germany that are outperforming the United States but also Finland, Korea, Iceland, and Poland.[4]

While this international testing has not received much attention in the United States, many other countries pay considerable attention to it, and they use the results to guide their needs for policy changes and educational improvement. Germany is a case in point. Even though its students regularly place higher than ours, the country as a whole has focused on student achievement, including both the distribution of outcomes within Germany and the comparison of German students to those in other countries. The release of international test results is the top story of the day in German news media. This attention to performance is entirely appropriate, as it puts pressure on German schools to improve and on politicians to seek ways to facilitate better schools.

It is possible to explain away part of the American drift toward the bottom of the achievement rankings. The United States does have a diverse student body with significant numbers of new immigrants and non–English speakers—but so do many European countries. The United States has long set the goal of educating all children to a high level, meaning that the United States historically has had broader enrollment in high schools, which statistically depresses average test scores. Yet today U.S. students graduate from high school at rates *below* the average of developed countries, implying that other countries are now providing more access to schooling than the United States—while still attaining higher average levels of achievement.

The conclusion is inescapable: The United States is simply not performing up to the educational level of many other countries, and this will have implications for our future economic success.

Policies Aimed at Inputs

So the big question is: How can we change this situation?

The simple position taken here is: *If one is concerned about student performance, one should gear policy to student performance.* It is not sufficient to focus on things we think or hope are going to be related to achievement.

But identifying the policies that will work to increase student performance isn't necessarily easy. In recognition of the importance of quality teachers, a variety of recommendations and policy initiatives have been introduced. Unfortunately, some of the most popular ideas are more likely to lower teacher quality than to improve it.

One idea that has been widely picked up by policy makers at all levels is to increase the requirements to become a teacher. The idea is simple: If we can insist on better prepared and more able teachers, teacher quality will necessarily rise, and student performance will respond. This argument—at least as generally implemented—proves to be as incorrect as it is simple.

The range of options being pushed includes raising the coursework requirement for teacher certification, testing teachers on either general or specific knowledge, requiring specific kinds of undergraduate degrees, and requiring master's degrees. Each has surface plausibility, but little evidence suggests that any of these is strongly related to teacher quality and to student achievement.

More pernicious, these requirements almost certainly act to reduce the supply of potential teachers. In other words, while the proposed requirements do little or nothing to ensure high-quality teachers, they do cut down on the numbers of people who might consider entering teaching. If teacher certification requirements end up discouraging potentially high-quality teachers who do not want to take the specific courses required, they behave less like a floor on quality and more like a ceiling.

These flawed teacher certification initiatives are actually just a special case of a larger set of misguided policies that go under the name of *input policies*. These are generally attempts to dictate specific pieces of the educational process and in effect to regulate higher achievement. They also include attempts merely

Table 1: Public School Resources in the United States, 1960–2007

	1960	1980	2000	2007
Pupil-teacher ratio	25.8	18.7	16.0	15.5
Percentage of teachers with master's degree or higher	23.5	49.6	56.8	n/a
Median years of teacher experience	11	12	14	n/a
Real expenditure/student (2007–2008 dollars)	$3,170	$6,244	$10,041	$11,674

n/a = not available

to provide more resources to schools without increasing any of the incentives to perform better.

The clearest example is found in the recent craze for lowering class size. For the decade before school budgets began to shrink due to the 2008 recession, class sizes generally were pushed down with no obvious effect on student outcomes.

The failure of class size reduction typifies the kind of input and resource policies that we have been employing for the past several decades. The evidence on these policies comes from a variety of sources but is very consistent—and damning. Table 1 shows the pattern of resources devoted to U.S. education since 1960. As is easily seen, there have been dramatic increases in what many people believe to be the most crucial educational resources—all of which well-meaning people continue to advocate increasing today. If we look at the years 1960 to 2007 (which roughly matches the relevant period for our data on student performance), we see that pupil-teacher ratios have fallen by 40 percent, the prevalence of teachers with master's degrees has more than doubled, and median teacher experience has increased dramatically. Since each of these inputs involves significant cost, average real spending per pupil has more than tripled—that is, it has increased by some 270 percent—after allowing for inflation.

NAEP Scores, 17-year-olds, 1971–2008

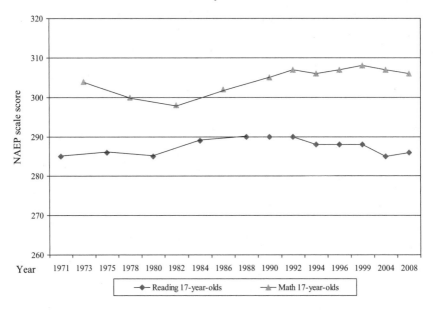

It is now useful to turn to Graph 1 (above), which tracks student performance on the National Assessment of Educational Progress (commonly referred to as "the nation's report card"). We see that the math and reading skills of seventeen-year-olds has remained virtually unchanged over almost four decades. This is hardly what the proponents of increased resources suggest should have happened.

These general findings on resources and performance are supported by detailed statistical studies of what goes on in the classroom, which adjust for differences in student background and the knowledge students bring to school. They provide little reason to believe that input policies will systematically improve student outcomes. While a few studies suggest positive relationships associated with added resources—which advocates of specific policies are quick to point out—they are balanced by studies that actually show *negative* relationships—which advocates never discuss. On balance, it seems clear that input policies do not offer a solution to the problem of stagnant or declining student achievement.

Furthermore, it is important to understand how pursuing the conventional input policies could actually *worsen* the situation. As pointed out, increasing the requirements for teacher certification could limit the supply of potential teachers and could thereby actually lower quality of the typical teacher who ends up in the classroom. Similarly, lowering class size could hurt in two ways. First, it is very expensive, so it absorbs funds that could be applied to other, more productive policies. Second, it expands the demand for teachers and therefore could lead to the recruitment of more low-quality teachers—which in turn could lead to lower student achievement.

Note, however, that we do not know much about the overall effects of class size reductions. The California class-size reduction policy of 1997 indeed drew in more teachers who were not fully certified, but it is unclear whether they were lower quality, because certification is not closely related to effective performance in the classroom.

The generic issue is whether higher levels of government can effectively improve schools by increased funding or uniform rules governing how education is to be conducted in local schools. Here the evidence is quite clear: We do not know how to identify a well-defined set of inputs that is either necessary or sufficient for ensuring high-quality schooling. Finding such a set of inputs has been the Holy Grail of education research, and the search has been quite unsuccessful. Indeed, I do not believe that it is an issue of just needing more or better research. I simply do not think we will identify such a set of "magic bullet" inputs with any clarity—at least, not within our lifetimes. I believe that the educational process is simply much too complicated for researchers to uncover a small set of things that are amenable to

central legislation and control that can make a decisive difference in the quality of educational achievement.

The evidence also underscores another aspect of the policy-
making problem. Class-size reductions have been very popular
politically. This helps to explain why other states and the federal
government soon began mimicking California's popular 1997
actions by funding class-size reduction programs. Much of this
political sentiment emanates from common-sense arguments
that persuade the general public—after all, doesn't it "stand to
reason" that a smaller class will allow the teacher to have more
intensive, and therefore more productive, interactions with each
student? It seems very logical—but it conflicts with the evidence.

The lesson is that the educational policy maker must deal
with political problems as well as policy problems. Parallel political problems exist regarding policies requiring master's degrees,
restrictions on who can get teacher certificates, and the like.
Policies that empirical studies show to be ineffective may
nonetheless attract significant political support, which makes
them very difficult for policy makers to resist.

Incentives for Performance

If input policies have failed to deliver improved student performance, what other kinds of policies can we examine for possible solutions to the problem? The most significant are policies
related to the structure of incentives in educational systems—
and of these, perhaps the largest problem with the current organization of schools is that nobody's job or career is heavily
dependent on student performance.

This is not to say that teachers or other school personnel are
currently misbehaving or ignoring the needs of students. Most
teachers are very hardworking and try to do the best they can in
the classroom. But like all human beings, teachers respond to

the incentives that are placed in front of them—and the current incentive systems used in public education do not make higher student achievement the chief objective. So when educational decisions are being made, they may or may not be guided by the goal of maximizing student learning. Instead, they may be directed toward options that are publicly popular or make the work of teachers and administrators easier or more pleasant.

The solution, of course, is to focus performance incentives for teachers and other school personnel on student achievement. The problem is that we do not know the best way to structure incentives. We have not tested many performance incentive systems in our schools, so we have very little experience with them and very little evidence as to which systems will produce the results we want.

A variety of approaches have been suggested, many of which have conceptual appeal: performance pay for teachers, rewards for high-performing schools, and various forms of parent or student choice, including charter schools, tax rebates, and vouchers. While evidence is slowly accumulating, the range of experiences is still very limited.

There are nonetheless some things we are quite certain about in the design of incentive structures.

One is that we want to reward a teacher for what she adds to a student's learning—that is, for the value she adds to the education of the child. As a corollary, rewards should be based on what teachers control, not the specific group of students they are given.

One reason for the general resistance by teachers and their unions to incentive systems such as performance pay is concern about what will be rewarded. As we discussed previously, we know that families make a huge difference in the education of students. One implication is that we should not reward or punish teachers for the portion of educational outcomes they are not responsible for. If some students come to school better prepared than others, their teachers should not receive extra rewards for the good results that background produces. Similarly, if students come from disadvantaged backgrounds that leave them less well prepared for schools, we should not punish their teachers.

Rewarding teachers appropriately in a complex situation like this requires an aggressive system of performance measurement that can separate the effects of classroom performance by the teacher from the influence of external factors that the teacher can't control. We have to be able to track the progress of individual students and relate this progress to the teachers who are responsible for it. This does not necessarily mean that we want a system of individual rewards as opposed to group rewards for teachers in a school, but it does mean that we have to measure school performance accurately. Nor does it mean that test-based measures should be exclusively used.

Accountability has become a contentious issue, especially when it is taken down to the level of individual teachers. The data on student performance provide valuable information on learning in different classrooms, but they are not the only information available. The tests do not cover the full range of influence of teachers or the full contribution of teachers to a school's success. Moreover, testing programs do not cover all the subjects and teachers in a school. Therefore, it is important to use other information from principal evaluations and, perhaps, the evaluations of other teachers.

This area of educational reform—designing accountability systems—is an obvious area for federal leadership (although not necessarily for federal control). Schools prepare people for future employment, but the free-flowing nature of society means that, say, a student educated in Georgia could well end up working in California. Thus, there is a national interest in ensuring that everybody has high levels of skills. Moreover, there is no need to reinvent the standards for and assessments of basic skills fifty times over. Recent efforts to develop common standards and testing across wider groups of states appear very sensible.

At the same time, the advantages of high-level decision making on the goals of education do not extend to specifying how to reach these goals. We also know that local decision making is crucial to designing effective incentive systems. It is almost inconceivable that we could run a good performance incentive system with regulations from the state or national capital. If we try to devise the "one best system" for the entire country and force it on local districts and schools, we will almost certainly fail. Local educational needs vary considerably, as does local capacity of the schools for implementing any programs or approaches. Developing a general set of rules for how best to educate children across the country's 14,000 school districts and 100,000 schools is simply beyond our capacity. What policies, for example, would simultaneously fit the one district with more than a million students and the 2,700 districts with fewer than 300 total students? While the federal government and state governments can help provide either funding or guidance on the use of performance incentives, they are not in a good position to determine *how* performance incentives should work.

At the same time, we should not simply assume that local districts and schools are currently able to make good decisions in this area. The personnel now in place were not chosen for their ability to design, operate, and manage different incentive systems. As mentioned, even specialists do not have sufficient experience to provide any detailed guidance. Nonetheless, preparing local officials for these tasks is where we should be headed.

Neither should we assume that every policy that emphasizes student outcomes and provides performance incentives is necessarily effective. The design of incentives is complicated, and many incentive structures lead to unintended and undesirable consequences. For example, if a move to broaden school choice heightens racial or economic segregation in the schools, most people would consider this an undesirable policy. We need to develop more experience with incentives and evaluate these experiences critically. With incentive systems, the details generally prove to be crucial.

The ultimate goal of the incentive systems we design must be to attract, encourage, and reward high-performing teachers while pushing low-performing teachers toward either improving their efforts (if they are capable of doing so) or leaving the profession altogether. Over time, the effect of such systems will be to greatly increase the number of good teachers while drastically reducing the number of ineffective teachers. In a reformed school system along these lines, the chance that a student can enjoy several successive years with an excellent teacher will be much higher. Reduced achievement gaps and heightened overall levels of accomplishment should be the result.

Some people think that improving the teacher force is almost impossible, because we have to live with the current teachers for years into the future. The truth is, however, that we currently have a large number of excellent teachers. At the same time, we also have a number of very ineffective teachers—teachers who are hurting students. If we could simply eliminate the bottom 5 to 10 percent of teachers (two or three teachers in a school with thirty) and replace them with average teachers, we could dramatically change student outcomes. This reform would ensure that the work of our good teachers would not be swept away by a bad teacher. Existing research suggests that getting this kind of small change would push the United States near the top of international rankings in math and science performance.[5]

A recent investigation of international achievement supports this simple idea. Specifically, one attribute of the best systems in the world is that—unlike in the United States—they do not let bad teachers stay in the classroom for very long.[6] We need to change incentives to get local schools to decide whether to retain teachers based on student achievement rather than other factors.

Finally, we need to think about the political context in which school incentives operate. Current school personnel are generally not interested in making large-scale changes in what they are doing. Thus, they do not support ideas about changing the compensation, tenure, and retention systems to reflect student performance.

This reluctance to embrace change is one of the strongest arguments behind expanded choice through charter schools or other options. If schools see that their effectiveness directly affects their ability to attract students—and thus to obtain funding—they have a strong incentive to do a better job, especially by ensuring that there are effective teachers in all of the classrooms.

Many people think of charter schools and parental choice as benefiting only those who are lucky enough to get into a good school. Those benefits are certainly real. Yet there is a larger benefit from putting pressure on the existing traditional public schools through the possibility that they will lose clientele if they do not perform well. Through this mechanism, charter schools and other alternatives can benefit all children, not just those who attend them.

Some Conclusions

Improving our schools is a policy imperative. The economic future of the United States depends crucially on the quality of our schools. Whether we continue to lead the world or our economy falls back depends on having a well-educated workforce.

Of course, we've known for half a century that U.S. schools need reform. We have responded by almost quadrupling our spending per pupil, but we have done so in ways that have not translated into achievement. It is clear that just putting more money into the existing system will not lead to significant improvements.

Extensive research on schools leads to a single conclusion. Student achievement is directly related to the quality of teachers. No other potential focus of school policy has anything like the effectiveness of policies that recruit and retain good teachers.

The details of how to ensure that we have effective teachers in all classrooms are still under study, but the general elements are clear. We have to focus incentives on student performance. We have to reward schools and teachers who promote high achievement—and not reward those who fail.

Three other elements seem important. First, we have to assess the value added of teachers and administrators. In other words, we need to focus on everybody's contribution to learning, and we need to hold everybody accountable for the learning gains they do or do not produce.

Second, we need to decentralize decision making so that local schools—where the demands are known, where the people are known, and where programs can be designed to increase achievement—have the freedom to perform. We cannot try to specify from the state or national capital how to learn.

Third, we have to offer school choice to all parents. Currently, well-off parents exercise school choice through their selection of residential location, but poor parents have many fewer options. Choice options such as those presented by charter schools help all families by putting pressure on schools to improve.

Some argue that it is just too hard to make big changes in our schools. Implicitly these people are willing to accept huge losses in the well-being of our children and in the health of our economy. There is strong public support for reform in our schools, and it is time to mobilize that support to restore the strength of our schools. In that, the focus must be ensuring a highly effective teacher in every classroom.

PART III

EMILY

INTRODUCTION

Emily's Story

Emily is an eighth grader in Silicon Valley. She lives in an affluent neighborhood with schools that boast high graduation rates. The local high school has golf and water polo teams, a state-of-the-art drama theater, and amazing test scores. She doesn't have to worry about her safety or a lack of resources, but she does have to worry about her academic future.

Emily doesn't want to go to her neighborhood school because the school tracks its students. So if Emily isn't considered to be as smart as another student, she will be placed on a lower academic track with fewer learning opportunities. Emily has trouble with math, so instead of working hard in her regular math class, she will be placed in a remedial course with worse teachers and lower expectations.

As *Waiting for "Superman"* begins, Emily wants to go to Summit Preparatory Charter High School, where there is no student tracking. Every student is held to the same set of high expectations, so Emily will learn more and improve her chances of getting into the college of her choice.

Emily is one of 455 applicants applying for 110 places at Summit. She has a 24 percent chance of being accepted. . . .

Calling All Citizens

Eric Schwarz

Eric Schwarz is the cofounder and CEO of Citizen Schools, a leading education nonprofit that partners with middle schools to expand the learning day for low-income children. Citizen Schools has been awarded *Fast Company*'s Social Capitalist Award and the Skoll Foundation's Award in Social Entrepreneurship. The organization serves 4,500 students and engages 3,800 volunteers across seven states and eighteen school districts.

Schwarz has served on the Massachusetts Board of Elementary and Secondary Education's Task Force on 21st Century Skills, the Center for American Progress working group on Expanded Learning Time, the transition team of Massachusetts governor Deval Patrick, and New Profit Inc.'s Social Entrepreneur Advisory Board. He is the author of the essay "Realizing the American Dream: Historical Scorecard, Current Challenges, Future Opportunities," published in 2005 by the Gathering of Leaders forum, and the co-editor of *The Case for Twenty-First Century Learning* (San Francisco: Jossey-Bass, 2006).

Previously, Schwarz served as a Public Service Fellow at Harvard University and vice president at City Year. Schwarz earned his bachelor of arts at the University of Vermont and his master's in education at Harvard University. He lives in Brookline, Massachusetts, with his wife and two children.

"There is a sleeping giant of education reform and it is us: average citizens from all walks of life. More than any new curriculum, new funding source, or new management plan, what students need is more attention, love, teaching and guidance from more adults. In our search for better outcomes for kids, we need to stop bashing schools. The rest of us need to pitch in."

The paragraph above is from "Citizen Schools," a concept paper I wrote in 1995 with my friend and college roommate Ned Rimer. We had our eyes on two great assets we felt could be at the center of the next wave of education reform. One asset was *time*. We never tired of telling people—and still don't—that children spend only 20 percent of their waking hours in school, and that the out-of-school experiences of poor and wealthier children are even more different than their in-school experiences. If we're serious about closing the achievement gap between advantaged and disadvantaged kids, we need to attack the time issue and find ways to make much better use of some of the 80 percent that is now largely wasted.

But more time for learning is productive only if it is filled with cool stuff—engaging and authentic activities that make learning relevant, rewarding, and fun. That's why the second asset we had our eyes on fifteen years ago was *talent*—specifically legions of national service corps members providing academic support, along with volunteer "citizen teachers": architects, chefs, engineers, filmmakers, and other professionals who could work hand-in-hand with classroom teachers to teach kids what they know.

Our concept paper led to the creation of the Citizen Schools organization. Fifteen years later, Citizen Schools is a leading practitioner and innovator of expanded learning programs.

Today, with those fifteen years in the rearview mirror, I appreciate that there are no "silver bullet" solutions in education.

But I remain convinced that if we are truly committed to dramatic learning gains for all children, then education reform must stop being a spectator sport. To turn around our schools and to restore the promise of education as an engine of opportunity for all children, we need to move millions of citizens off the sidelines and into the game as tutors, mentors, citizen teachers, PTO/PTA members, education activists, and even micro-philanthropists.

This chapter makes the case that you and your friends—in your role as ordinary citizens—have a direct and substantial role to play in making America first in education again. We can't wait for Wendy Kopp or Michelle Rhee or Bill and Melinda Gates to fix our education system; we need to join them and get busy doing it ourselves.

Redefining Teaching

My mother was a ninth-grade English teacher who worked in New York City's East Harlem neighborhood, across town from where we lived. As a preteen I remember visiting her classroom and marveling at her ability to engage her class in real-world projects, such as creating a professional slide show documenting the school's neighborhood. Some of her students read at just a second-grade level and many had significant challenges at home, but Mom didn't let these challenges discourage her. She worked late into the night customizing lessons for them and was dedicated to building esprit de corps across her classroom.

I was moved to start Citizen Schools in part because I wanted to be a teacher like my mother. But I didn't want to do it full-time. One day back in August 1994, I came up with an idea that would let me step into a classroom without making a full-time commitment to the teaching profession. I contacted my friend Nydia Mendez, principal of Dever Elementary School in Boston's Dorchester neighborhood, and asked if I could work with some of her students to publish a newspaper. I had worked as a daily journalist and columnist for five years and I thought teaching journalism could be my way to connect with kids—and to test the idea for Citizen Schools, which was already percolating in my mind. Nydia gave the green light, saying she knew just the right fifth-grade teacher who would be happy to have me teach half of her kids a few hours a week.

That fall I spent twelve two-hour sessions with ten fifth graders writing and editing the *Dever Community News*. I remember nervously making last-minute adjustments to my lesson plans as I walked to my class from the train station near the school, the hulking *Boston Globe* newsroom behind me and the Dever fifth graders ahead. I wasn't a great teacher, but the kids thought it was a great class. I was a real editor, and they became real journalists.

Every kid in the apprenticeship wrote at least two published articles. They edited one another's work and were edited by me as well. We sold $400 worth of advertisements to local businesses. We had comics and a crossword puzzle. And one day in our last week together, we all piled into a rented van and drove to a printing press in Chelsea, a small city across the Mystic River from Boston. We watched in awe as our paper flew off an old printing press that folded the papers, stacked them in bunches of five hundred, and wrapped the bunches tightly in plastic twine. When we got back to Dever, the kids walked a little taller as they distributed their newspaper to classmates and teachers. I like to think they wrote a little better too—not just for this project, but for all their classes.

As for me, I was hooked. And Citizen Schools was born.

Citizen Engagement as
a Driver of Educational Success

Since 1995, Citizen Schools has recruited and trained more than 10,000 volunteers to do the same thing I did at Dever. They teach from the textbooks of their lives and lead short courses that culminate in an authentic and joyful product. We call our volunteers citizen teachers, and we call the ten-week courses they teach apprenticeships. Our students have learned an amazing array of skills from citizen teachers. They've worked with Google's best and most-tattooed young engineers to design video games, and they have worked with amateur and professional astronomers to measure the heavens.

There's no "typical" citizen teacher, but the story of Dave Mantus exemplifies the excitement our volunteers bring into classrooms around the country. A PhD chemist with Cubist Pharmaceuticals in Lexington, Massachusetts, Dave has vivid childhood memories of doing science experiments in the backyard with his father and grandfather. Those experiences instilled in Dave a true passion for science that led to his studying biomedical engineering at the University of Washington and chemistry at Cornell University.

Dave began volunteering with Citizen Schools after hearing about the desperate need to give kids more hands-on learning activities to get them excited about learning, specifically around science. For two years now, through Citizen Schools, Dave has been teaching rocket science to middle school students one afternoon a week.

He calls his course "It IS Rocket Science!" and he gives students the chance to do things they miss out on in their traditional science classes. Dave drags all kinds of gear into the classroom for eye-popping science experiments each week. The kids have launched rockets from their school parking lot and presented ideas to Cubist's CEO on bringing a drug to market. They've even been to Dave's office building for a live video conference with NASA.

The students have a blast and they learn a whole lot along the way. None of the students Dave is working with have a PhD chemist in their family to do experiments with them in the backyard. But now these students do have the opportunity to work with Dave once a week and experience his contagious passion for science.

Supporting and complementing the volunteer citizen teachers, Citizen Schools also recruits and deploys hundreds of full-time teaching fellows—recent college graduates supported by the AmeriCorps national service program who lead academic and enrichment activities. The teaching fellows and the volunteer citizen teachers work together to extend the school day from six to nine hours, four or five days a week, for the entire school year.

And they generate strong results. We've completed two rigorous evaluations that have confirmed the benefits the Citizen Schools program brings to schools. We've seen more than 30 percent reductions in absenteeism and suspensions, double-digit gains in proficiency rates in math, science, and English, and a 52 percent increase in high school graduation rates.[1]

Citizen Schools isn't the only organization mobilizing volunteers to improve education. Many outstanding charter schools recruit and deploy volunteers and national service members, like the Match Corps members who provide one-on-one tutoring to students at Boston's Match School in the afternoon and evening. After-school and summer programs such as BELL, Breakthrough, College Track, Higher Achievement, and more achieve strong results by deploying nontraditional teachers to support traditional public schools.

One particularly impressive effort is Experience Corps, a national program to recruit retirees to volunteer in elementary schools. A recent experimental study that looked at more than eight hundred second and third graders at twenty-three high-need schools in three cities concluded that over a single school year, students with Experience Corps tutors made 60 percent more progress in learning critical reading skills than similar students not served by the program.[2]

Collectively, these education support programs and the citizens who are their lifeblood should be seen as a front-burner school improvement strategy—not an afterthought or a distraction, as many education reformers have claimed. Well-structured and well-designed citizen engagement in schools produces stunning results.

Still, I feel as if we are sitting on a gold mine and are just barely beginning to mine it.

What if the nation could mobilize 1 million—or 10 million—citizen teachers? What if these millions of scientists and artists and businesspeople and filmmakers could teach the skills they know and love to children, whether during or after school? What if these citizen teachers made learning more fun, more relevant, and more impactful for tens of millions of children?

These questions are bubbling up in an environment ripe for innovation and fundamental change. Now seems like the time to dream big. National efforts such as Race to the Top and the Investing in Innovation (i3) Fund are prompting the nation to take a hard look at how we educate our students and what we need to do to increase student achievement. The issue of time has moved into the spotlight thanks in part to consistent mentions by President Barack Obama and Secretary of Education Arne Duncan. Across the country, legislators, school districts, nonprofit organizations, and teachers' unions are beginning to look at education reform differently and question long-standing assumptions. If we take full advantage of this environment, we have an opportunity to effect real change right now before it is too late.

Concerned citizens can play an enormous role in this reform effort.

A "Second Shift" of Educators

Nationwide, there are 3.5 million classroom teachers tasked with teaching the country's 56 million K–12 students. It falls on these teachers to teach reading, writing, and arithmetic, as well lessons in science, civics, music, art, sports, and dozens of other subjects. These same teachers also try to serve as tutors and mentors and try to prepare their charges for higher education and the workforce, struggling against long odds to impart core academic skills as well as life skills, self-esteem, and strong character.

Not surprisingly, the system isn't working. National education outcomes are stagnant despite a doubling of our national investment in education over the past thirty-five years. It's not necessarily that the current teachers are doing a poor job, although a small number clearly are; many of the country's public school teachers and principals are skilled and hardworking. Most are good people doing good work. The fundamental problem is the assumption that 56 million public schoolchildren—almost half living in or near poverty or in homes where English is the second language—can be adequately prepared for life by 3.5 million teachers in just thirty hours a week, thirty-six weeks a year.

In his new book *Education Unbound*, Frederick Hess writes about rethinking our approach to education reform.[3] He asserts that by "scrubbing away our assumptions about districts, schoolhouses, teacher training, and other familiar arrangements," we can look at education reform with a fresh perspective on the best ways to use resources, such as time, talent, and technology. In a section titled "Rewriting the Job Description," Hess outlines how schools might do a better job of utilizing talent and cites Citizen Schools as an example of how schools can tap skilled volunteers.

What if we were to take on Hess's challenge to let go of our assumptions and rethink what it means to be a teacher? What if we invite different adults to teach different material in different ways at different times during a child's day? And what if we use the enormous intellectual and social resource represented by concerned citizens to create a powerful "second shift" for education that extends the school day and gives kids vastly expanded opportunities to learn and grow?

As we rethink our education delivery system, we need to learn from other fields of practice, such as medicine. Although the delivery of medical care in America is far from perfect, it does illustrate how practitioners with different forms and levels of experience and skill can collaborate to meet the diverse needs of diverse "clients."

For example, an experienced physician often spends only a few minutes with the typical patient, allowing and empowering junior clinicians who have appropriate skills and training to make routine decisions about treatment and to speak more extensively with the patient. This approach allows the senior physician to spend more time on the most challenging cases and to train and mentor younger providers.

I recently broke my finger playing basketball. When I went to see the doctor for a critical follow-up visit, I noted that I spent twenty minutes with the nurse, ten minutes with the X-ray technician, seven minutes with the orthopedic resident, and then just two to three minutes with the doctor I had come to see. The combination of talents, expertise, and communications styles provided by these several professionals gave me a more effective healing experience than any single practitioner could have created.

When it comes to education, we might not want to follow this structure exactly, but we could take some lessons from the physicians' playbook. Indeed, we can try to change the ideal image of the teacher from that of soloist—even a virtuoso—to choreographer, bringing together people and resources in different combinations to create a vibrant learning environment that is enriched by real-world skills and caring relationships.

For example, nine to ten hours of organized instruction for a student might include four hours with a "master teacher" (a highly trained professional), two to three hours with a "teaching fellow" (a young educator or mid-career switcher), and an additional two hours with a community volunteer (a coach, citizen teacher, or online educator who facilitates distance learning).

In New York's Chinatown, Joel Rose is overseeing a pilot program, the School of One, that uses a mixture of teachers, graduate students, high school interns, and technology tools, such as computer worksheets and virtual online tutoring, to deliver instruction. By broadening the definition of "teacher," the program makes it possible to tailor daily lessons and activities to individual students' strengths, weaknesses, and interests. The model focuses on universally high expectations for all students, at the same time that it frees students to learn in different ways at varying paces. Adding more adults to the mix makes it all possible.[4]

At the Met School in Providence, Rhode Island, where more than half of the students qualify for free lunch and 42 percent come from homes where English is a second language, students are asked to identify their passions, then meld them into internships and substantive projects that serve real-world purposes. The school relies heavily on community volunteers for the rich, real-world learning opportunities its students enjoy. And the program works, with virtually all Met graduates going on to college.[5]

Schools that partner with such organizations as Citizen Schools or Experience Corps, or adopt a design such as the Met School, do better in part because they offer students what some educators call the new 3 R's: more *relationships*, more *relevant* learning projects, and more time for *rigorous* practice and skill building. But sociologist Robert Putnam says these schools are successful for an additional reason—they have more of what he calls "social capital," the web of mutual commitments and networks among citizens who know one another. Putnam's research, included in his seminal book, *Bowling Alone*, concludes that social capital has a significantly larger impact on student performance than does overall school spending, parent income, or parent education levels.[6] That's right: By engaging parents and other adult volunteers in a school community—even a very low-income school community—schools can create a support system that reinforces and builds upon the work of teachers and overcomes the challenges of poverty.

From Soccer to Science: How Citizen Teachers Can Help Lead a Learning Renaissance

Citizen Teachers represent a new and counterintuitive strategy for improving public schools. But in a different arena they are a resource the nation is already tapping—in significant numbers and with significant effect. Coaches of youth sports teach millions of our children how to play soccer, baseball, basketball, and other sports. The school in Brookline, Massachusetts, that my children attend offers physical education twice a week for forty-five minutes. The physical-education teacher, Mr. Hutch, is excellent, but his time on task pales beside the hundreds of hours of basketball and soccer instruction that my son and daughter receive from volunteer coaches in multiple leagues.

Mr. Hutch plus citizen teachers make for a great combination. For millions of children, the same is true for education in music, theater, and art. Professional and certified music, theater, and art teachers in schools provide a fraction of the teaching provided by noncertified teachers outside of school.

A few decades ago, the United States didn't even compete worldwide in soccer, and youth soccer leagues were rare. Now the U.S. men's team is a legitimate international contender, and the women's team is a powerhouse. U.S. professional soccer teams now play in front of crowds in excess of 60,000. Soccer is gaining popularity and our national level of play has improved markedly. Did this happen because we hired a battalion of certified, professional soccer teachers? No, we're getting much better at soccer because 900,000 volunteer coaches are sharing their knowledge, their commitment, and their time with millions of children. These coaches, mostly moms and dads of players on their teams, have varying skill levels but they play a critical role in advancing learning about soccer. Their work allows a much smaller number of expert teachers (paid soccer coaches) to focus their attention where they can have the greatest impact—in this case, on higher-level teams and on developing players with extraordinary interests and talents.

If volunteers can help lead soccer (and baseball and basketball) instruction for millions of children, it's not far-fetched to imagine volunteers improving science teaching and learning in our schools. President Obama has seized upon this opportunity, calling on the nation's 5 million professional scientists, including 200,000 who work for the federal government, to get engaged in classrooms and help bring science to life through real-world projects and experiments. The president's science adviser, John Holdren, has notably said:

We wouldn't teach football from a textbook. It is even more important that America's youth have the opportunity to learn math and science by doing. The president and I strongly support efforts to raise the level of project-based learning, to help cultivate the next generation of doers and makers.[7]

The Edgerton Center at the Massachusetts Institute of Technology has conducted research indicating that 85 percent of middle school children are interested in science but that two-thirds of them believe they will not pursue careers in science because either they don't know any scientists or they don't know what scientists really do.[8] Citizen Schools is increasingly focused on mobilizing scientists and engineers and technology professionals to become citizen teachers (Dave Mantus, whom we cited earlier, is a great example).

The White House is supporting National Lab Day, an exciting new effort to further this cause. Led by software entrepreneur Jack Hidary, National Lab Day has created a sophisticated online database that matches teachers who want to work with a scientist and scientists who want to work with kids. If we could recruit just 2 percent of the nation's 5 million scientists to volunteer with schools, we would provide one scientist volunteer for every certified science teacher at the middle and high school levels.

Volunteers can't, and shouldn't, replace trained teachers in the classroom. But just as in youth sports, there is ample room for them to support and complement the work that expert, professional teachers do.

The Apprenticeship Model

The core of the Citizen Schools model is our apprenticeship approach to teaching. For most people, the word "apprenticeship" probably conjures up the old-fashioned image of a young boy toiling in a blacksmith's shop, gradually learning the trade. Others may think of the apprenticeships trade unions offer, such as those for electricians or carpenters. At Citizen Schools, we have a different approach to apprenticeships that is based on educational research and successful results with our students.

What most traditional apprenticeships and Citizen Schools apprenticeships share is a teaching style that involves showing the "apprentice" how to perform a task, having him or her practice it with the help of an expert instructor, and then providing "scaffolding" and feedback that allow the apprentice to start doing the task independently. While traditional apprenticeships focus on immediate job training, Citizen Schools apprenticeships are designed to highlight potential career paths and to connect those future possibilities to students' current learning and to college.

One student who attended our program—I'll call him John E.—was referred to us by his mother because he was struggling in school. John grew up in Boston's Dorchester neighborhood. He had a learning disability, his classes didn't seem relevant to him, and his grades were mostly C's and D's. These were the facts presented in his school profile. But there were other facts, and these we learned by getting to know John and his family. John loved animals. He befriended injured birds and stray cats he found near the apartment complex where he lived. Once, he'd even found a wounded bat and nursed it back to health at home without his mother ever knowing.

At Citizen Schools, John took an apprenticeship called Drugs on the Brain, taught by Marcus Delatte, a postdoctoral researcher at Harvard Medical School. Marcus had grown up in New Orleans and was drawn to the Citizen Schools program by the chance to give back to kids who shared a background similar to his own. In the apprenticeship, John had the chance to hold a human brain in his hands. He dissected a sheep's brain and conducted experiments, adding droplets of alcohol to a slice of the brain tissue and using a microscope to observe and record the reactions of the brain cells. That's how science became real and relevant for him.

John had always wanted to be a veterinarian. Now he learned that becoming a veterinarian required years of biology coursework and that future study in biology would be aided by his current work in math and science classes. John is now a senior at one of Boston's best high schools and has joined mainstream classes in math and science, earning a B average. He is in the process of visiting colleges and plans to be either a veterinarian or a marine biologist.

For thousands of years, people have learned by doing, through hands-on experiences. But it was educational philosopher John Dewey who originally advocated for learning by doing in the classroom. Later, psychologist Jean Piaget researched and wrote about the "concrete operational stage" of learning where children begin to make abstract connections based on concrete experiences. More recently, Columbia University scholar Lauren Resnick has argued that one of the key features of programs that teach thinking, learning, or higher-order cognitive skills is that "they are organized around joint accomplishment of tasks, so that elements of skill take on meaning in the context of the whole." The apprenticeship model harnesses all of these concepts in the service of concrete educational achievement.

Learning through apprenticeships is theoretically possible in traditional schools powered entirely by full-time certified teachers. But it's a lot easier for a school to employ real-world apprenticeships if it has real-world experts who can help do the teaching.

Stop Waiting for *"Superman"*

The last generation of education reform has focused on three priorities: teacher quality, testing and accountability, and charter schools. These initiatives are all important, and valuable progress has been made in each area. But if we want to design education policy based on actual results, we must also acknowledge that although we now have almost 5,000 charter schools, a decade of test scores and accountability ratings, and a generation of alternative teacher recruitment and professional development strategies, today our high school graduation rate is lower than it was a generation ago and by most measures education outcomes have been stagnant. America's place in international rankings of academic skills and educational attainment has dropped from near the top to below the middle among industrialized nations.[9] The Obama administration has good ideas for fine-tuning our national pursuit of teacher quality, charters, and testing and accountability strategies, but in my view, these approaches alone are unlikely to deliver sustainable and substantial improvement for all children. Citizen involvement is the missing ingredient that can help make all the other elements of school reform more effective.

Citizens can remake education in America by getting involved by the millions in five specific ways:

1. Sign up as a mentor or tutor at Experience Corps (www.experiencecorps.org), Big Brothers/Big Sisters (www.bbbs.org), or any of the hundreds of additional well-structured tutoring and mentoring programs and help one child master math or navigate early adolescence.

2. Become a citizen teacher at Citizen Schools (www.citizen schools.org) or through National Lab Day (www.national

labday.org) and share your passion or profession for a few hours a week, complementing traditional education by leading a real-world "apprenticeship course" for children.

3. If you are a parent, get active in your child's school, including joining the PTO or PTA. Did you know that PTO membership has declined from 47 percent to 19 percent of public school parents over the past fifty years?[10]

4. Read this book, see the movie on which it's based, and then activate. Organize a book group around the theme of education reform. Meet with your local elected representative and advocate for more results-focused education funding.

5. Become an educational philanthropist. Check out www.donorschoose.com to make a donation to one of thousands of real-time educational projects that teachers need your help to complete. Find an education nonprofit that works and focus your philanthropy on helping it grow.

From the citizen soldiers who fought for independence to the citizen activists who fought for civil rights, America has met its biggest challenges when its citizens get directly involved. But for too long citizen leadership and direct citizen involvement have been absent in education. All our children need and deserve networks of adults who see their full potential and are dedicated to helping them succeed. Now, at a moment of urgent need and great opportunity, it's time to open the schoolhouse doors wide to welcome in new talent and fresh thinking. The millions of citizens with talent, energy, and passion to share are a great place to start.

PART IV

ANTHONY

INTRODUCTION

Anthony's Story

Anthony is a fifth grader in Washington, D.C. He attends one of the worst-performing school districts in the country, but he's a good student and he studies hard.

Anthony didn't always enjoy school. He never knew his mother, and after losing his father to drugs in 2004, he acted out in class, didn't care about grades, and had to repeat second grade. He moved in with his grandparents, who provided more discipline, and with a good teacher, Anthony began to study, pay attention in class, and turn his grades around. But next year he will move up to a struggling middle school where students fall two to three grade levels behind.

Anthony's grandmother knows how difficult it will be for him to succeed at the school and worries about his safety. Anthony's neighborhood is plagued by crime, drugs, and violence. Anthony needs a way out.

One school can offer him that opportunity. SEED Charter School is one of the few public boarding schools in the country and it produces remarkable results. At SEED Anthony would move out of his troubled neighborhood and into a challenging academic environment where nine out of ten students go on to college. But with sixty-one applicants for twenty-four spots, Anthony has less than a 50 percent chance of getting into SEED. . . .

Putting Kids First

Michelle Rhee

Michelle Rhee was appointed chancellor of the District of Columbia Public Schools, a school district serving more than 47,000 students in 123 schools, on June 12, 2007.

Chancellor Rhee's commitment to excellence in education began in a Baltimore classroom in 1992 in the Teach For America program. At Harlem Park Community School, she learned the lesson that informs her work every day: A city's teachers are the most powerful driving force behind student achievement in a school.

In 1997, Rhee founded The New Teacher Project (TNTP), a leading organization in understanding and developing innovative solutions to the challenges of hiring new teachers. As chief executive officer and president, Rhee partnered with school districts, state education agencies, nonprofit organizations, and unions to transform the way schools and other organizations recruit, select, and train highly qualified teachers in difficult-to-staff schools.

Her work with TNTP implemented widespread reform, improving teacher hiring practices in Atlanta; Baltimore; Chicago; Miami; New York; Oakland, California; and Philadelphia. Since 1997, TNTP has placed more than 23,000 new, high-quality teachers in these schools across the country.

———————————

When I took the job of chancellor of the District of Columbia Public Schools, only 12 percent of our incoming high school students could read on grade level, and only 8 percent were on grade level in math.[1] Just 9 percent went on to graduate from college within five years of high school graduation.[2] In math we had achievement gaps at the secondary level of 70 percentage points between black and white students, and 79 percent of our students are black.[3] When compared to other urban school systems with similar demographics, our kindergartners started off relatively on par with other districts, but they started to fall behind within three months.[4] Judging by the sole function of a school system—to give children the skills they need to become productive members of society—it was clear that the system in Washington, D.C., was broken.

Too often when we talk about fixing broken school systems, we focus on what adults think. But I have found that the best ideas come from the kids in our schools. When I was asked to write about "Putting Children First," I decided to let them show you what they have shown me over the past three years.

Here is what I have learned from our students: Children want a great education. They know when they are not getting it. And when we offer it to them, they will go after it with everything they have.

Far too many people are under the misconception that we can't have high educational expectations for children who live in low-income neighborhoods. But the children are proving that this just isn't true. There is no doubt that poverty presents real challenges, and it is harder to be a principal or teacher in an urban district than it is in the suburbs. But even in the toughest of neighborhoods and circumstances, children excel when the right adults are doing the right things for them.

In fact, when children even just *begin* to get what they need from their schools, they themselves begin to drive change and hold themselves to high expectations.

One of our schools, Sousa Middle School, is in one of the highest-poverty wards in the city. Three years ago it was one of our most struggling schools. The lights were broken and graffiti covered the walls. Kids ran through the hallways and skipped classes with impunity. Fewer than 16 percent of the students could read and do math on grade level. No wonder the federal government had flagged Sousa as a failing school that needed a complete overhaul.

So we aggressively recruited and hired Dwan Jordon, a young assistant principal from a neighboring school district. He had never been given the chance to run a school, so it was a risk to put him in charge of one of our toughest middle schools. But when my team and I interviewed him, we saw something in him that convinced us to take the risk. We thought this was a person who would get things done by the sheer force of his will. We were struck by his strong vision and his obvious personal commitment to kids.

Once the school year started, I began to hear about good things happening at Sousa. Parents said Mr. Jordon was bringing order and discipline to the school, and that things were changing for the better. But it was not until the end of the year, when we saw what had changed in student achievement, that I was truly astounded. Mr. Jordon had created color-coded levels of achievement for the children, making it easier for them to set goals and move from "below basic" (red) to "basic" (yellow) to "proficient" (green) to "advanced" (blue). The system worked. In just one year under Mr. Jordon's leadership, Sousa gained 17 percentage points in reading proficiency and 25 in math, meeting federal benchmarks for progress for the first time in Sousa's history. This means that Sousa more than doubled its student proficiency rate in math and increased its proficiency rate in reading by 70 percent.

These kinds of gains are unheard of—especially for a first-year principal in one of the toughest middle schools in the city. This was so astonishing that I had to visit the school myself to see what was going on.

When I toured the new Sousa, I was amazed. The building was immaculate. The hallways were orderly and the kids were all in uniform according to Mr. Jordon's new policy. In every class I entered, 100 percent of the kids were engaged. Unlike the same kids a year earlier, they had no hoods on their heads and no earphones in their ears. I almost didn't recognize the place.

I scheduled a time to talk with the teachers a few days later. When I arrived for our meeting just as school was getting out for the day, the kids ran up and surrounded me, welcoming me to Sousa with calls of "Chancellor Rhee, Chancellor Rhee!" or "How are you, Chancellor Rhee?" or "I am only two points from being proficient!"

Usually kids don't recognize me. They often ignore me or ask, "Who is that Chinese lady?" But here, they came at me from all directions, excited, happy, and proud to greet their chancellor.

It's not that recognizing me means students are doing well in school. In fact, this wasn't about me at all. But the fact that the students knew who I was and what the district's expectations were told me that the adults in that building had made them feel both a sense of individual responsibility for success and an investment in the shared mission of the school and the entire district.

I asked one sixth grader, "What elementary school did you go to before Sousa?" He told me, and I asked, "Do you feel that school prepared you for the rigors of Sousa?"

"It's different," he said.

"Why?"

"The teachers here *teach*." *Ugh*, I thought. That wasn't what I wanted to hear about the other school.

"What do you mean?" I asked.

"Here they push you—you know, to think outside the box."

After talking with students, I went inside for my meeting with the faculty. I frequently hold listening sessions with teachers and can usually tell within a few minutes what the vibe of a faculty is: their energy level, their attitudes . . . they say a lot before a single word is spoken. This group was clearly very anxious, and I assumed they were wondering about the purpose of my visit, so I wanted to allay their fears from the beginning.

"Look," I said, "you are doing a tremendous job here. I have been so impressed by what is happening here at Sousa. I just want you to know that I don't expect to see 20 percent increases in achievement this year after you pulled off such huge gains last year. We will all be disappointed if the kids lose ground, but a 4 or 5 percent gain per year would be terrific."

The response surprised me. "Let me tell you one thing," one teacher said. "The horse is out of the barn for the students in our school. Our motto is 'Striving for excellence,' and our students will not be satisfied with a 4 percent increase. *They* are aiming for the blue! *They* want 20 percent gains, and they're not going to be satisfied with anything less! You can't even give them a worksheet anymore. They hold us to delivering an engaging lesson every single day."

We then had the kind of discussion that is exactly what a superintendent would want to have with a faculty, focused completely on what the teachers could do best for the kids. They asked about lesson plans, resources, strategies, and teaching methods. We had made some controversial decisions recently that had garnered a lot of coverage in the local news media, but I didn't hear a single question about them. They were too on fire about teaching to worry about anything else.

I was thinking I would relieve their anxiety. I was wrong. They were nervous, but not about pressure from the chancellor—they were worried about living up to the expectations of the kids!

Now that the students had a great principal and committed teachers to lead the way, they were coming to class, wearing uniforms, and having *fun* working hard. They'd started to compete with themselves and aim for high goals. With their teachers they'd mapped out how to reach those goals, and they were eager to check their progress along the way. Some of them were even going to school on Saturdays—voluntarily—to do extra work they knew they needed.

And if you think that it's just the younger students who seize onto this kind of educational opportunity, it's not. If you ask most people in the country, they don't say the nicest things about teenagers in Washington, D.C. Yet those teenagers are some of the most impressive people I have ever met. From the day I arrived, they have been telling me they are not getting the education they need from our schools and asking for more challenges.

I once met with a group of students from Anacostia Senior High School, located east of the Anacostia River in one of the city's lowest-income wards. I had heard all the stereotypes and complaints about students in this school. According to most reports, they were naturally truant and prone to violence, basically bad kids with little interest in learning.

Nothing could be further from the truth. They were more organized and professional than some of the adults I had met with the same day! They had a full agenda with a list of items they wanted to discuss. They were respectful, but insisted on a serious, meaningful discussion about what I was going to do to improve their school. And they knew exactly what they wanted from me: "Offer us the same Advanced Placement courses that students get on the other side of the river." "Make our school look less like a prison." "Make our school safe."

I worried about disappointing them. Their wish list was long, and they had limited time left in the system. Some of the items they wanted we could deliver on right away, but the more complex items would take some time. I didn't want to make promises I couldn't keep.

I asked them, "If you had to pick one thing I could do to make this a better school for you, what would it be? What is the most important change you want to see?"

"Great teachers," they said unanimously. "Bring us more great teachers."

Since then, almost every conversation I have had with students has led to this reasonable request.

Students are very serious about wanting to learn from the best. During an unannounced visit to one high school, I noticed that many classrooms were nearly empty. I saw only one that was full, an English class in which the students were actively engaged in discussion. As I left the school an hour later, I noticed that three young men who had been in the English class were leaving as well.

"Where are you going?" I asked one.

"We came to school because the first-period teacher is a good one," he said. "The second isn't, so we're rollin.'"

People think kids are truant because they don't want to learn. But this story shows that a lot of students are making informed decisions. They are going to the places where they know they will get the education they deserve. If our public schools don't measure up, the students will walk away.

Students make these kinds of decisions all the time. We heard of one situation in which a teacher had too many students in her class. She had kids showing up every day who weren't even on her roster. Some of them had taken her class already, and others just weren't registered. At first we thought it was some problem with the way students were assigned. But when we talked to the students, it turned out they were in her class because they knew the teacher was good. They wanted to learn, and they knew they could learn in her classroom. They didn't even care that they would receive no credit for the class.

Not only are students making calculated choices to seek out learning, they are asking good questions about why they are not getting challenged like this in every classroom. One group of kids from one of our most struggling high schools came to me after participating in a summer learning program. They had researched Advanced Placement (AP) course offerings across the school system, and for their final project they had compiled the data, analyzed it, and formulated recommendations for improvement. They identified a pattern showing that in our school district, students who live "east of the river" have historically been offered far fewer AP courses than their peers at public high schools "west of the park." They finished their presentation by asking me to explain the reasons for this pattern.

"Why aren't these AP courses offered in our school? Is it that nobody thinks we can do the work?" they asked. And, "Is it because we're poor, Chancellor Rhee? Is it because we're black?" Make no mistake, young people are ever cognizant of racial inequity and the low expectations set for them, and we too often underestimate the power that these low expectations have over their lives.

Small meetings like this made me realize that students were giving me some of the best insights into the school system available anywhere. In response, I started a monthly meeting with a student cabinet composed of students recruited from every high school in the school system, so I could hear more. They did not disappoint me. In one of our first cabinet meetings, the topic of low expectations came up. One student brought up the media.

"It's no wonder everyone thinks we're all thugs," he said. "Look at all the stories they choose to tell about us—it's all crime, drugs, and violence. Why do they only report the bad things about us?"

"Let's ask," I answered.

I invited a reporter who covered the school district to come to our next cabinet meeting and talk to the students. I have to give her credit for acknowledging and responding to the students' anger at the media, despite the fact that she herself is a pretty fair and thorough reporter.

One student pointed out, "Last year there was a fight at our school, and the press was all over the place. But did you know that two weeks earlier, we had the highest number of students on the honor roll the school ever had? Where were you then?"

Another student chimed in, "That kind of reporting sends all of us the message that bad behavior is what is expected of us. That only contributes to the problem and makes more of us go in that direction." They were respectful, but they pressed her pretty hard. They were so clear and forceful that I wished every reporter who covers us could have been on the hot seat of accountability that day!

The reporter was honest in return and explained that the emphasis on bad news was about selling papers and the newspaper's need to survive as a business. Knowing how powerful an impact the message of low expectation has on children's lives, it was frankly depressing to hear. But at least she was straight with them. We underestimate students any time we think we can fool them about anything, especially the expectations we harbor for what they will be able to accomplish.

Students will meet the low expectations of someone who doesn't think they will amount to much. But by the same token, they can tell when they meet someone who has their best interests at heart, and once they know that, they will work as hard as they have to in order to meet the high expectations that person sets—through words, actions, time, consistency, and example. This doesn't mean our students are angels, and sometimes teachers have to reassert those high expectations—and their unyielding belief that the students can meet them—every day, even in the face of setbacks and disappointments. But when a school is staffed by a team of adults doing this together, children show us the rewards by meeting high expectations at every turn.

One of the places I saw it happen this year was at Shaw-Garnet-Patterson Middle School under the leadership of Principal Brian Betts. We had lured Mr. Betts away from a very successful school district in the area to lead two struggling urban schools we were merging into one. Neither school had met federal performance baselines for years.

Mr. Betts changed all that. From day one, Mr. Betts was on the corner every morning and in all kinds of weather to greet students. They knew not only that they were welcome but that they would be missed if they weren't there. He learned every student's name and became a mentor to many of them. In his first year, he sent personal notes on all three hundred report cards going home. He challenged kids to meet high expectations and would not let them settle for anything less.

A group of eighth-grade boys at Shaw-Garnet-Patterson found that for the first time they could remember, they actually were excited to get up and go to school every morning. They felt the change from the year before, appreciated the kind of education they were getting with Mr. Betts as their principal, and worried that they would not get the same education when they moved on to high school. So they petitioned me to let about one hundred eighth graders stay at Shaw for the ninth grade. They knew about the performance data for the high schools around them and laid out their own performance goals, arguing that they could reach them with Mr. Betts as their principal.

Adding a high school grade just for one group of students wasn't an easy thing to do. As a management decision it didn't actually make much sense. But the students convinced me that they would do whatever they needed to in order to make it work. In the end, I said yes, but I stressed, "It is *only* for this year." They agreed.

The next year, I hadn't seen them for a while when Mr. Betts called to say that they missed me and wanted to talk about how things were going. I visited the school for lunch with a group of students, and they told me about their work, their teachers, their progress toward their academic targets, and their lives in general. As I was picking up my lunch tray and moving to leave, I wished them good luck in the tenth grade.

"Speaking of the tenth grade . . . ," one student began.

"No!" I interrupted. "Remember our conversation last year? I agreed to let you stay here for the ninth grade—and the ninth grade only."

They pushed back, and I realized I'd been set up. I called Mr. Betts, and he fessed up—and presented his plan. He wanted to turn the school into a 6–12, and he laid out how and why he should be able to do it. His dream was to send all of his students to college straight from Shaw.

When we looked at the whole district, including the feeder patterns of middle schools into high schools, the idea just didn't make sense from an administrative perspective. But once again, he got me in the end. I thought, giving students more time to learn with Brian Betts as their principal will make it worthwhile to grow Shaw into a 6–12. It was the topic of our last conversation.

Sadly, just a few days later, Mr. Betts was killed by an intruder in his home. Dealing with that tragedy has been one of the most difficult things I've had to do as chancellor. Brian Betts was the real thing—the kind of person who doesn't come along very often.

The story of the eighth graders at Shaw vividly illustrates that despite the stereotypes people try to pin on our students, they are hungry for a great education and will pursue it when they see it. After Mr. Betts's death, this group of kids has only impressed this upon me more.

Mr. Betts's body was found the night before a school holiday, but the kids gathered at school the next morning because they had heard the news. Of course, they were terribly upset.

They hugged me, they cried, they asked me, "Who would want to hurt Mr. Betts?" (A subsequent investigation showed no connection between the death and either the students or the school.) A few of the ninth graders asked what would happen to them and the school next year now that Mr. Betts was gone. I said we would work it out and that we would talk about it with them when things had calmed down.

Weeks later, I visited the school and asked the students, "So what should we do?"

They were all in agreement. They wanted to stay.

I knew I had to be honest with them. "Here's the story," I said. "The numbers might not work. We need a minimum number of students to make the school expansion viable. What are students saying? How many ninth graders do you think will stay without Mr. Betts here?"

One said at least seventy, but one little girl shook her head at that. She thought half would leave. It became clear that we had a problem, as half the kids thought we should abandon the 6–12 idea, and the other half thought we should keep it.

Two students said they didn't want either option. They wanted to stay for their tenth-grade year, then go on to high school. I didn't understand how this would be good for them. I asked, "But if you know you're going to leave after the tenth grade, why not transition now? Do you want to be transitioning to high school halfway through?"

One responded for them both. "We are very clear on what Mr. Betts's vision was and what his expectations were. And we know we are close to achieving that vision, but we are not there yet. The tenth-grade year is our testing year." (He was referring to the D.C. Comprehensive Assessment System, which is a local test given in grades three through eight and ten.) "That means we'll have one more year to reach the goals we set. We can show what we wanted to show from the beginning. Everyone who thought we couldn't do it will see what we can do. We'll have the data to back it up. We'll close out Mr. Betts's vision."

I was floored. For ninth-grade kids to have put all those pieces together in this way within just a few weeks of Mr. Betts's death was to live out this man's legacy.

We're still wrestling with the difficult decisions this tragedy has forced upon us. But regardless of what we ultimately decide about grade configurations, the students' story is testament to the fact that when you do the right things for kids, when you hold high expectations and give them the tools to meet those expectations, they will do phenomenal things.

Shaw and Sousa are not the only schools in which great principals have begun to turn things around. But in every school where it happens, I invariably hear the same thing from kids when I ask how things are going.

"It's harder," they say.

"Is that good?" I ask.

"Yes," they say.

"Why?" I ask.

"We're learning. Last year we ran around in the halls and did everything we weren't supposed to do. It was chaos."

"And how is it different now?"

"We can't get away with that anymore!"

It is practically the same conversation every time.

Educating students the right way isn't easy. In fact, it's incredibly difficult work and it takes strong leaders to do it, but at the end of the day, when we guide children in the right way as adults, children of *every* background will go in the right direction. In just two years in Washington, D.C., secondary students have reduced the black-white achievement gap by 20 percentage points in math. In 2007, only 24 percent of African-American elementary students in D.C. were proficient in math. By 2009, that had jumped to 42 percent.[5] Clearly we still have a long way to go, but students are progressing faster than ever.

It's also happening among Hispanic students, who represent 12 percent of our student body. Compared to students in other urban districts, 40 percent of Hispanic fourth graders in our school system were at the basic level or above in math in 2003. [6] By 2009, they raised that number to 69 percent. Both low-income and Hispanic fourth-grade students in D.C. led the nation in gains.

Compared to other urban districts, D.C.'s children ranked number one in growth for the first time, increasing their scores at a higher rate than any other tested urban district in the country.[7] Our fourth and eighth graders have never grown at this rate, and they are racing to catch up and surpass the expectations set in more affluent districts than ours.

We've come under fire for a lot of things over the past three years, from incorporating teacher performance data in layoff decisions to "moving too fast" on all kinds of reform. Many people have said we should have tried harder to build consensus and rely on collaboration to reform the school system more gradually. But show me the parent who wants his or her child to wait in a subpar school while we work slowly and collaboratively to fix it. From negotiating union contracts to rewriting policies and firing underperformers, far too often in public education we have been willing to turn a blind eye to what's happening to kids so we can avoid making waves. We can't do this anymore. We can't allow another generation of kids to fall by the wayside while we take our time trying to build consensus in the interest of harmony among adults. That isn't going to happen on my watch.

It is not too late to listen to the kids. They know very well when they are being shafted, and as educators we should be accountable only to them. If we base our decisions on what they need, we will change the face of public education across the country. Every single child will receive an excellent education, and documentaries like *Waiting for "Superman"* will no longer be necessary.

Five Foundations for
Student Success

Randi Weingarten

Randi Weingarten is the president of the 1.5 million-member American Federation of Teachers and the former president of New York City's United Federation of Teachers. A former history teacher at Clara Barton High School in Brooklyn's Crown Heights neighborhood, Weingarten helped her students win several state and national awards debating constitutional issues.

Weingarten has launched major efforts to place education reform and innovation high on the nation's agenda. She has advocated a number of flexible, proactive approaches to improve teaching and learning, including a new template for teacher development and evaluation; a fresh approach to due process for misconduct cases; ensuring teachers have the tools, time, and trust to succeed; and forging collaborative labor-management relationships. More than fifty AFT local unions and their district partners have begun work on new systems to develop and evaluate teachers based on the AFT model.

Since becoming AFT president, Weingarten has been personally involved in helping several AFT affiliates achieve innovative, reform-minded collective bargaining agreements.

She also initiated the AFT Innovation Fund, supported by AFT member dues and substantial grants from private philanthropic organizations, to help AFT affiliates develop innovative, bottom-up reform projects with their district partners.

I respect what Davis Guggenheim and his team set out to do in their film *Waiting for "Superman"*—to show how far we are from the great American ideal of providing every child with the excellent education they need and deserve.

As I watched *Waiting for "Superman,"* I didn't see just the stories of Anthony, Francisco, Bianca, Daisy, and Emily. I saw the stories of millions of children, millions of parents, who know that education—public education—is their path to opportunity. I saw that for myself in the schools I attended in Clarkston, New York. I saw that every day I taught history in the Crown Heights section of Brooklyn. And today I see it as I visit schools all over the country.

For me, the challenges laid bare by this film hit home so powerfully because I know how widespread and complicated they are. So while it was incredibly moving, and at times upsetting, to watch the stories of these five children unfold, I found myself thinking again about what we must do to guarantee a quality public education for all children—not for 5, or 500, or even 5,000 children. But how we can finally, successfully realize the fundamental right of *every* child—the right to an education that prepares them for a fulfilling life.

That right is denied too many children, an injustice we all must work to rectify. The essential value of public education is to prepare today's students to be not only tomorrow's workers, but also to be the caretakers of our environment, the tenders of our global relationships, the creators of our arts, and the innovators of enterprise. But even more fundamentally, public schools educate our children—all children who walk through our doors—because every child has the right to a fair and hopeful start in life.

Ninety percent of American students—nearly 50 million children—attend our public schools. Change in a single classroom, a single school, or even a single school district is not enough. Our enterprise is not a niche business. Reforms that affect small numbers of students, even when they live up to their promise, still leave a promise unfulfilled for the vast majority of students who attend our public schools.

Those are the students entrusted to our care in the public schools. We don't select them. We don't turn them away. We educate them, and we seek the tools, resources, and supports to educate them at the highest levels.

Many public schools are meeting this challenge. I've seen successful strategies at work in schools all across America. And yet, creating both the will and the strategies to ensure that we can replicate success eludes us. This film may help with the first, but we need concrete steps to accomplish the second.

What's heartening to me is that in the schools I have visited—schools often wildly divergent in everything from geography to demography—there are five recurring elements that foster educational success. I've outlined them below.

Before getting to those, let me say that I understand that a film needs to have a compelling story line, replete with good guys and bad guys. But teachers and their unions are not the bad guys. The millions of hardworking, dedicated teachers in America's classrooms see a different story than the one told in *Waiting for "Superman."* Teachers struggle mightily to help their students make progress, often hindered by systems that lack the collective will and in some cases the collective capacity to do the right thing for all of our kids. We can help facilitate progress, not impede it.

When we define the challenges more broadly, we see the solutions more broadly, too. That's why I appreciate the opportunity to add my thoughts to the others shared in this volume, because I believe there are many areas where we can trade contentiousness for collaboration and help America's teachers to be the change agents they want to be and our students need.

Much of the tension in this film stems from whether the children featured will get the chance to attend the school their parents seek for them. The fact is that the opportunity to access a great public education should come not by chance, not by choice—but by right. We should applaud schools that produce great student achievement in difficult environments. But, fundamentally, this is why islands of excellence will never be enough. In the end, no solution is as scalable, as accessible, or as accountable as a great neighborhood or regional school. Such a school is both an accessible opportunity for students to learn, and a stable force for the community. Parents should have choices, and one of those choices should be a public school that provides the kind of education that opens doors throughout our children's lives, and that is also safe and accessible.

That is a national as much as a neighborhood obligation, which is why this film's portrayal of teachers and the unions that represent them as emblems and agents of the status quo ignores the fact that teachers—as much as or more than any "reformer"—are confronting each day the challenges their students face.

Many of those who weigh in on the state of our public schools do so from an ivory tower, a think tank, the opinion pages, or from in front of a television camera. Teachers have no such remove. They are in classrooms every day, seeing what their students need, and doing the hard work to help them succeed. They are daily change agents.

Teaching is complex work. I often think of the words of the psychologist Lee Shulman, who wrote of teaching:

> Even when working with a reading group of 6–8 students, teachers are overseeing the decoding skills, comprehension, word attack, performance, and engagement of those students while simultaneously keeping tabs on the learning of the other two dozen students in the room. The only time a physician could possibly encounter a situation of comparable complexity would be in the emergency room of a hospital during or after a natural disaster.

He concluded that classroom teaching "is perhaps the most complex, most challenging, and most demanding, subtle, nuanced, and frightening activity that our species has ever invented."

As you read this, more than 3 million public schoolteachers are working in classrooms around the country to master this challenging activity, helping young minds embrace new facts, new skills, new ways of thinking.

To characterize the vast majority of those teachers as defending the status quo not only is flat wrong, but it also creates a diversion that impedes us from actually changing a more broadly defined status quo.

On top of the fact that, even in the best of circumstances, teaching is complex work, requiring skills to differentiate instruction to students' needs, there are other societal and economic facts that can't be ignored.

One example is the 12 million children who come to school hungry, in which case the "job" of the teacher also includes slipping the student a granola bar or a couple of dollars so he can think about something other than the gnawing pain of hunger in his belly.

Some factors come from within the school, such as un-healthy, crumbling buildings and outdated textbooks. And some factors are broader failures of the systems entrusted with supporting education, such as funding shortfalls, ballooning class sizes, and a severe shortage of guidance and counseling services for students. Or an overreliance on narrowly focused and poorly designed tests that should never substitute for a robust curriculum, but instead too often serve as a de facto curriculum.

Unfortunately, *Waiting for "Superman"* focuses on two kinds of outliers: bad teachers and difficult-to-replicate schools, the implication being that if you get rid of a few bad teachers and create a few boutique schools, you can solve all the problems of education. You can't.

Because if that is all you do, you're still just continuing to wait for a *"Superman."*

Follow the film to its logical policy conclusion, and the message is, we're waiting for *"Superman"* to arrive in the form of 4 million iconic teachers to replace the ones we have today. We're waiting for *"Superman"* to arrive in the form of 96,000 iconic principals to replace the ones we have today. And we're waiting for *"Superman"* to arrive in the form of 15,000 iconic superintendents to replace the ones we have today.

Well, while we're waiting, there are 49.5 million students in our public schools who need and have the right to a great education, an education that will enable each one of them to make the most of their potential.

We need real solutions that can work for the vast majority of American children who are educated in our public schools, and can work for them not ten years from now, but now.

Doing this requires that we lay five foundations for student success:

1. Good teachers supported by good leaders
2. Good curriculum
3. An environment that eliminates barriers to student success
4. Shared responsibility and mutual accountability
5. Collaboration, not competition or combativeness

Here's what I mean by each.

Good Teachers Supported by Good Leaders

Good teaching is central to improving public education. But speaking from my own experience, there are very few teachers who are great teachers on their first day in a classroom.

There has been a lot of talk about teacher quality, and about who is a "good" teacher and who is a "bad" teacher. Much of this talk seems to fall back on the assumption that teachers enter the profession as either one or the other—good or bad—and stay that way. The truth is that while wanting to teach may be innate, becoming a great teacher is a learned skill. The key is creating the educational infrastructure that helps all teachers strengthen their skills.

Teacher evaluation can help play that role, but too often, instead, it is a sorting exercise—not so much an opportunity to strengthen teacher practice. Evaluations should serve both purposes—to gauge *and* develop teacher effectiveness.

Today this is how teachers still are commonly evaluated: by an administrator sitting in the back of the classroom for a few minutes, a few times, in the first few years of teaching. The teacher then receives feedback at the end of the semester or the end of the year. It's like a football team watching game tape only when the season is over.

An effective evaluation system is continuous and comprehensive. It enables teachers to review their game tape and share what matters when it matters—when there's still time to remedy short-comings or to build on approaches that are working. It deconstructs what works and what doesn't, rather than simply offering a snapshot from a brief classroom visit or one standardized test score.

We need ways to develop and evaluate teachers that will lead to continuous improvement.

The American Federation of Teachers has done just that: developed a new way to evaluate teachers' performance and to help them improve their practice. It involves rigorous reviews by trained expert and peer evaluators, based on professional teaching standards, best practices, and student achievement. The goal is to lift whole schools and systems: to help promising teachers improve, to enable good teachers to become great, and to identify those teachers who shouldn't be in the classroom at all.

Our framework has been developed by union leaders from around the country, with input from some of America's top teacher evaluation experts.

Our evaluation proposal includes the following key components:

- Professional teaching standards that make clear what a teacher should know and be able to do

- Methods for assessing teachers' performance according to those standards

- Systems of support that help all teachers grow professionally

- A fair and expedient process to remove from the profession teachers who do not improve

Between January 2010, when this framework was announced, and this writing, more than fifty districts and their unions have embraced the framework, and that number is growing. AFT unions are partnering with school districts to transform teacher evaluation from a perfunctory waste of time into a powerful catalyst for student achievement.

And teachers will tell you that their ability to help their students is magnified when they have the support of good leaders. Principals, assistant principals, and administrators are charged with instructional support—at their best they help teachers grow in their profession, ensure the necessary resources and supports are in place, and allow teachers to teach. During school and after school, teachers and administrators are forging partnerships for student success.

Unfortunately, *Waiting for "Superman"* does not include any of the numerous teacher-led efforts to strengthen teaching and learning. Instead, the film's seminal image of a teacher is a twenty-two-year-old example of one teacher in one school in Milwaukee who shouldn't be in the classroom.

That may be compelling filmmaking, but it's certainly not a remotely accurate (or fair) characterization of the more than 3 million public schoolteachers in America.

No teacher—myself included—wants ineffective teachers in the classroom. Schools are communities where we build on one another's work. When a teacher is disengaged or floundering, there are repercussions not only for the students, but also for the teachers down the hall, who take responsibility for those students the next year. When it comes to those teachers who shouldn't be in the classroom, other teachers are the first to speak up.

And that's why we have worked to develop a way to develop and evaluate teachers that is an achievable, sustainable, and fair way to ensure that we have a qualified teaching force. We don't want to be waiting for *"Superman."* But when the facts are depicted otherwise, it simply demoralizes every good teacher who is working incredibly hard to help our students learn. They must be celebrated, not vilified, even as we do what we must to make systemic changes to ensure all students have great teachers.

In fact, our own experience shows us just how flawed it is to think that simply removing poorly performing teachers, rather than focusing on systemic changes, will help all kids.

Several AFT unions have taken the lead in helping struggling teachers improve, and when those teachers do not make adequate progress, they are counseled out of the profession. The first and most established program of this kind is in Toledo, Ohio, where the union instituted a program called Peer Assistance and Review.

Under this system, every new teacher is assigned to work with a consulting teacher, typically someone who teaches the same subject and grade level and evaluates the new teachers. Toledo's consulting teachers aren't rubber stamps. Based on the consulting teachers' assessments, between 8 percent and 10 percent of new teachers opt to resign or don't have their contracts renewed.

In May 2009, I visited Toledo to see several teachers making final appeals to have their contracts renewed. It was a scene as powerful as any in *Waiting for "Superman."* Like the kids in the film, these teachers were waiting to hear their fate. And they were let go, not by administrators but by their colleagues trained and selected for this work.

The AFT also has led the way in developing a fair, efficient protocol for adjudicating questions of teacher discipline and, when called for, teacher removal. As I write this chapter, this protocol is being developed by Ken Feinberg, who currently serves as special master of the September 11th Victim Compensation Fund and administrator of the fund to handle claims from those harmed by the 2010 BP oil-spill disaster, and is trusted as a voice of fairness and reason for some of the most consequential questions in our national life.

Finally, the United Federation of Teachers in New York City has reached an agreement whereby New York's reassignment centers, which are seen in the film and are known more commonly as "rubber rooms," will be permanently shuttered. This is one area where what is presented in the film is not documentary, but history.

Yet, as research, practice, and common sense demonstrate, none of these programs—impressive as they are—will singlehandedly raise student achievement. That's why the other foundations are important.

A Good Curriculum

So what is it that good teachers need to create the opportunity for students to learn? It begins with a good road map to learning—a good curriculum.

One of the consequences of No Child Left Behind (NCLB) is that what gets tested drives what gets taught. As a result, NCLB has put a premium on test-taking—specifically, learning how to bubble in multiple-choice answers in reading and math. In 2007, the Center on Education Policy surveyed a nationally representative group of school districts and found that 62 percent of them had increased the time devoted to reading and mathematics, while 44 percent reported that they had reduced the amount of time spent on science, social studies, and the arts.

So even if students score well on the tested subjects (mainly reading and math), have we really equipped them to compete in a world and in workplaces where higher-order skills like problem-solving and project-based learning are most valued? And what about how we inculcate a love of learning, or simply an engagement in schooling? There's no way our students can become the thinkers, innovators, and leaders of tomorrow if they have exclusively been "taught to the test," and taught only the subjects tested.

That is not good enough. Students need rich, well-rounded curricula that ground them in areas ranging from science to the arts, history to government. Curricula should focus not just on content in key subject areas but also those higher-order skills such as critical thinking that are so necessary for college and career, and so vital to creating a new generation of inquisitors and innovators.

A strong curriculum also provides the sheet music off of which teachers can create "variations on a theme"—different ways to reach different students with different strengths and interests.

I often think about a street law class I taught, in which, once I knew what concepts I wanted to get across, I let my students choose what to focus on. Having a say in their learning got them incredibly engaged and reinforced the importance of the interplay between a goal-oriented curriculum and the freedom for teachers to "differentiate instruction" or, in other words, to find ways to get their students to that goal.

Finally, curriculum should be matched with appropriate materials, supplies, books, technology, and enrichment opportunities that help learning come alive. It seems a straightforward thing to say, but it is shameful how many schools lack even those basic materials, much less coherent curricular materials that are common throughout a district or state, which teachers and students can use as a road map. All too often teachers still must make it up—that is, when they are not forced to simply teach to the test.

An Environment That Eliminates
Barriers to Student Success

The reality remains that family socioeconomic status is still the number-one predictor of student achievement, and roughly two-thirds of academic achievement is attributed to out-of-school factors, such as hunger, poor health, and difficult family circumstances.[1]

So how can we create an environment that eliminates barriers to student success?

Geoffrey Canada has taken this on and, in many ways, the changes made by the Harlem Children's Zone are a testament to its success. I admire and respect what Geoff has accomplished. But the movie draws the wrong conclusions from his work. The lessons come not from comparisons between charter and neighborhood schools but from the cradle-to-college services the Harlem Children's Zone provides.

The most comprehensive national study of charter and traditional public schools found that most charter schools perform worse than—or only about as well as—the public schools they are meant to supplement or supplant. [2]

So what makes the Harlem Children's Zone different? It's the services: the early childhood, family, community, and health services that envelop the schools and their students in an environment that prepares them for school and then helps parents reinforce the skills learned in school. (There's a reason the *New York Times* calls the Harlem Children's Zone "one of the most ambitious *social-service* experiments of our time" [emphasis added].)

These services don't come cheap. The budget of the Harlem Children's Zone is $36 million a year. Only one-third of that funding comes from the government.[3]

We need to find ways to provide similar services in all the places where the needs are just as great, but where $24 million in private donations—each year—is impossible to come by.

It isn't easy, but it is possible. I know this because I saw something similar in Syracuse, New York, and in Taylor, Michigan. And I saw it again when I visited John A. Johnson Elementary School in St. Paul, Minnesota. To give you a sense of the students they serve, this is a school where more than 90 percent of the students qualify for free or reduced-price lunch.

Johnson is a community school that works hard to get the important pieces in place—great teachers and staff, strong curriculum, fun and engaging activities for summer and for after school, and an amazing array of services that remove barriers to success for the kids and their families.

The school offers free space for organizations that bring their services to the school, housed in a wing connected to the school building. As a result, children and their families can walk into their school and find health and dental services, family and emotional support, housing assistance, early-childhood learning services, food and clothing assistance, employment aid, adult language instruction, and a full YMCA all just a corridor away.

It's a comprehensive, but by no means effortless, delivery. Teachers and specialists work hard in tandem so that when it comes to supports, it's not a confusing tangle but a seamless tapestry.

These and other in-school services are more important now than ever before. Since work began on *Waiting for "Superman,"* America's cities have seen the sharpest increase in the demand for hunger assistance since 1991—an increase driven by the number of middle-class families who are now seeking assistance from food pantries. Similarly, the sharp rise in homelessness has been driven not by individual homelessness, but by family homelessness.[4]

According to the Foundation for Child Development, the effects of the current recession will effectively wipe out thirty years of social progress in combating poverty and increasing community safety and family stability.[5]

This all means that more students than ever before are coming to school from unstable home environments and they're arriving hungry. Too many students right now lack the basic nutrition and health services to be alert and productive in and out of school.

My point is not to bemoan these challenges, but to point out that public schools must address them and, in many cases, provide children refuge from them and the skills to overcome them. And when we see places where wraparound services allow children and families to thrive—whether we find those examples in the Harlem Children's Zone or St. Paul, Minnesota, we need to figure out how to replicate that success.

Shared Responsibility/Mutual Accountability

We also need to recognize that while so much educational progress takes place in those important hours when a teacher and the subject matter and the student come together and the spark of learning can catch light, teachers and students are not the only people involved in our nation's public education system.

We need true accountability, accountability that is meant to fix schools, not to affix blame, accountability that takes into account the conditions that are beyond the teacher's or school's control, and accountability that holds everyone responsible for doing his or her share.

Principals, administrators, policy makers—all of these people have a role to play as well.

We believe that holding teachers solely accountable for student achievement is only partial accountability. We want to see that everyone whose actions and leadership (or lack thereof) impact education is held accountable as well.

Consider that half of all teachers leave the profession within five years. It's costly and counterproductive to hire thousands of well-qualified people every year—only to see so many leave within a year and more than one of every three by the end of the third year. Worse, it's bad for kids.

Should administrators be evaluated on creating schools with great teacher development and retention? I think so.

Isn't it tantamount to educational malpractice to hire teachers and leave them hanging? Isn't it ludicrous to lose so many potentially great teachers before they get the experience and support to actually become great? Isn't the loss of so many potentially great teachers as much of a concern as that of "bad" teachers? Yet this enormous, persistent problem is overlooked by policy makers and in this film.

We know that schools excel when all of the adults in the school—teachers, parents, and administrators—work together as a team, with a laserlike focus on student achievement and student social development. Shouldn't teamwork for student achievement be measured as part of full accountability?

And shouldn't accountability be a two-way street? Departments of education should be responsible for providing the necessary resources for a school to succeed. Are there enough teachers so that the school can maintain appropriate class size? Are there sufficient custodial services for the school? Is there an adequate supply of textbooks? Is the school equipped with science labs? Computers? A library? Is the department making sure the school provides meaningful, effective professional development for the school's staff?

In places where everyone is willing to take responsibility, we've seen some amazing progress.

I think of the ABC Unified School District in California, where the superintendent's cabinet and the union's executive board hold joint meetings to chart a course forward together. Initially the meetings were about an operational agenda—how do we make this system work? Today those meetings are about an instructional agenda—how do we make this system work for kids?

As a result, issues that might be contentious are handled collaboratively. Labor and management look out for each other to such an extent that while most California school districts are about to be decimated by layoffs, there will be none in the ABC district.

More important, student achievement is way up. The ABC district is an area with students from families with great wealth, as well as great want. Because there's true shared responsibility for results and collaboration focused on effective strategies, the schools are closing long-standing divides, and educationally, there's no wrong side of the tracks anymore.

And that's what this is really about. When there is true 360-degree accountability, everyone is accountable for his or her contribution, everybody is accountable to each other, and most important, everyone is accountable to the students—top to bottom and bottom to top.

Collaboration

Finally, we need to see one another as partners in the shared enterprise of shaping our future.

Just as with shared accountability, in schools and districts where true partnerships are in place, we've seen dramatic changes that benefit children.

For example, in New York, the AFT and Green Dot charter schools have a contract that is thirty pages long, about one-eighth to one-tenth the size of a typical district contract. It focuses on common goals and reform initiatives and embeds shared responsibility as an operating theory rather than attempting to anticipate and regulate everything that happens in a school.

Partnership is also the foundation in New Haven, Connecticut, where district and city leaders and the union engaged in a collaborative process. At the end of the process, Mayor John DeStefano Jr. admitted that at the beginning, he had been ready for conflict: "We thought about shoving it down the teachers' throats." And then, he said, "it [became] a matter of not doing it to them."

The stakeholders in New Haven's public schools worked toward a contract that achieves real reform—and makes teachers a partner in that effort.

The agreement includes such reforms as tough and fair evaluations, more flexible hiring authority, and fewer job protections for struggling teachers who fail to improve.

Like a number of AFT districts, New Haven has instituted performance pay for teachers on a schoolwide basis. This will allow them to do more than create pockets of excellence, class by class, but rather to develop schools of excellence, where everyone works together to make sure everyone improves.

By creating incentives for the team, instead of individual players, schools build camaraderie and, we think, achieve better results.

Ultimately, schools that succeed are built on collaborative, trusting relationships. They don't wait for "*Superman*"; they create environments where ordinary, devoted people can work together to collaboratively achieve extraordinary things on behalf of children.

Conclusion

Every child has a right to a great public education that prepares him or her for success throughout life. No one—certainly not those of us whose life's work is in education—is satisfied with the current state of education. We must focus our efforts to improve public education—not for the few, but for the many—and not as we know it now, but as we know it can and must be.

Working as a team, focusing on the development of great teachers supported by good leaders, using robust curriculum, and ensuring we eliminate obstacles—that's a prescription for success. And if we're able to put these things in place, our children won't need to wait for *"Superman"* or anyone else, because they'll have the tools and the talents to shape their own futures.

That's the message I take from this film. It creates a call to action, but rather than stop at whom to blame, or to hope and pray we once more find *"Superman"* or any other mythical solution, I hope that instead it facilitates a conversation about how we can guarantee children a great education—not by chance, not by choice, but by right.

That's a story I'd love to see in all of our schools—and on the silver screen—in the future.

PART V

BIANCA

INTRODUCTION

Bianca's Story

Bianca is a kindergartener in Harlem, New York. She goes to a Catholic school because her mother, Nakia, worries about sending her daughter to the nearby public school.

Nakia is a single mother and pays $500 a month for Bianca's tuition. She is a receptionist but is having trouble finding steady work. Recently her hours were cut back, so she can no longer afford Bianca's tuition.

Nakia didn't go to college and says she won't let her daughter make that mistake. She wants Bianca to get an education so she can have a career instead of a job, an opportunity Nakia missed. Even though Bianca must change schools, Nakia made her a promise: Bianca won't get everything she wants, but she will get everything she needs.

That's why Nakia has submitted Bianca's application for a spot at Harlem Success Academy, a free charter school with remarkable teachers and excellent test results. Bianca is one of 767 children vying for 35 spots—which means she has a 5 percent chance of getting in. . . .

What *Really* Makes a Super School?*

Jay Mathews

Jay Mathews is the education columnist at the *Washington Post*, where he has been for thirty-nine years. He attended Occidental and Harvard colleges and served with the army in Vietnam. He has reported from China and California, and covered the stock market in New York. He has written seven books on topics such as China, disability rights, the famous Los Angeles math teacher Jaime Escalante, and the lack of challenge in American high schools.

Mathews's rating system for U.S. high schools, the Challenge Index, appears every year in *Newsweek* and the *Post*. It has been cited in hundreds of newspapers and magazines since 1998 and got more than 21 million page views its first week on Newsweek.com in 2010.

Mathews's best-selling college admissions book, *Harvard Schmarvard* (New York: Three Rivers Press, 2003), shows why admission to a brand-name school will *not* change your life and instructs applicants in surviving the application process with their family and their sense of humor intact. His book *Supertest: How the International Baccalaureate Can Strengthen Our Schools* (Chicago: Open Court,

*Some of the material in this chapter originally appeared in a slightly different form in the *Washington Post* and on its web site, www.washingtonpost.com.

2006), describes the International Baccalaureate program's success in transforming ordinary schools, particularly Mount Vernon High in Fairfax County, Virginia.

His most successful book is his most recent, *Work Hard. Be Nice: How Two Inspired Teachers Created the Most Promising Schools in America* (Chapel Hill, NC: Algonquin, 2009). This story of how the KIPP schools raised the achievement of impoverished students to unprecedented levels was a *New York Times* best seller.

Mathews has won the Education Writers Association National Education Reporting Award and the Benjamin Fine Award for Outstanding Education Reporting, as well as the Eugene Meyer Award, the *Washington Post*'s top honor for distinguished service to the newspaper. In 2009 he received the Upton Sinclair Award for being "a beacon of light in the realm of education."

When writing about schools, even very good schools, I try to avoid using the word "miracle." It is the clunkiest cliché in the education writer's vocabulary, used too often and invariably incorrectly. But what I saw three decades ago in a small classroom at Garfield High School in East Los Angeles turned out to be pretty close to miraculous, at least in the sense of being totally unexpected and far beyond the range of normal experience.

A rumpled educator named Jaime Escalante, with a heavy Bolivian accent, was teaching math. Once I got a good look at what he was doing, I turned my back on my career as a national correspondent for the *Washington Post* and chose instead to return to local reporting, focusing on education.

At the same time, once other teachers and education policy makers digested the results of Escalante's math program, many became convinced that American educators had been greatly underestimating the capacity of inner-city students to master such difficult subjects as calculus.

Just one statistic tells the story. In 1987, fully 26 percent of all Mexican-American students in the United States who passed an Advanced Placement calculus exam were at Garfield High School. That means Escalante and the calculus teacher he trained, Ben Jimenez, were doing something extraordinary. It also means that hundreds of thousands of low-income students in schools *other* than Garfield were being deprived of the sort of teaching that could have prepared them for college and successful careers in math, science, and engineering.

What were the Garfield teachers doing that worked so well? In Davis Guggenheim's film *Waiting for "Superman,"* Harlem education entrepreneur Geoffrey Canada talks about the search for some superhuman entity to save our urban schools. Jaime Escalante was no *"Superman,"* but what he was doing had that otherworldly effect.

I have since tried to figure out what that was. How do you create not only a super teacher, but a super school? In the pages that follow, I'll share some of what I learned.

In the past ten years, experts have gotten closer to the formula. The charter school movement, an effort to create thousands of independent public schools free of the interfering annoyances of big school district bureaucracies, has been called an incubator of super schools. Some of the best charter schools, such as Geoffrey Canada's Harlem Success Academy or the Knowledge Is Power Program (KIPP), have produced results that almost match Escalante's. But the vast majority of charters have gotten nowhere near that level.

Paul T. Hill, director of the Center on Reinventing Public Education at the University of Washington, Bothell, explains this in his book *Learning as We Go: Why School Choice Is Worth the Wait* (Stanford, CA: Hoover Institution Press, 2010). Hill still believes charters are a worthy experiment. They are more promising, he says, than other reform ideas. But they have flaws that keep them from realizing in every case their advocates' hopes and expectations.

First, they are hard to run. "Principals from district-run schools are often not ready to make the financing, hiring, firing, admissions, and self-assessment decisions that fall on them" when they move to charters, Hill says. "Some learn, but others don't."

Second, charters are demanding places to teach. Teachers who move from regular to charter schools "become partners in an enterprise that must sink or swim depending on performance," Hill says.

Third, charters also can't compete successfully with district-run schools unless they get as much money for the pupils they educate. Given the politics of big-city school systems, that is not likely to happen in most cases.

Finally, charters are hard to reproduce, even when particular schools—such as the Harlem Success Academy or KIPP—are successful and well-known.

So yes, the charter school movement is part of the answer to the quest for the super school. But all of us—charter school leaders, parents, citizens, and policy makers—need to understand their limitations and challenges as well as their promise.

• • •

Are parents the answer?

Some political activists I respect say super schools can arise only if they have the full support of the local community. In 2010, one California group, the Parent Revolution, persuaded the state legislature and the governor to give parents a legal right to change their schools' leadership, even if their school district doesn't want them to.

This "parent trigger" plan has been sharply criticized by teachers' unions. The president of the California Federation of Teachers called it a "lynch mob" provision. Although now law, the parent trigger process will take time to develop because it is so complicated. If a school's average test scores are low, parents may circulate a petition demanding one of a set of options set out in the law, including closing the school, turning it into a charter school, or firing or reorganizing the staff. If 51 percent of the school's families, or 51 percent of a larger group of families whose children are on track to attend the school, sign the petitions, the change takes place unless the school district can persuade the state to choose a different option because the parents' solution is impossible or harmful. The law says no more than seventy-five schools will be subject to the trigger in California.

Jumping over all those hurdles will likely be exhausting and discouraging for even the most motivated parents. Parent Revolution spokesman Gabe Rose told me he thought that was good because it means no change will occur "unless there is broad parental consensus." But the difficulties increase the chances that parents will adopt unfortunate tools of American politics, such as distorting data, ignoring contrary information, and offering material inducements. Factions will almost certainly arise among the parents, as they do in all governing bodies. At the end of the process they are likely to be even more cynical and disheartened about our education system than they already are.

So my vision of a super school starts not with parents, but with teachers. After following scores of schools trying to improve, I have discovered that if the teachers do their job and raise students to new levels of learning, the parents will follow.

• • •

I learned this truth from Dave Levin, one of the founders of the KIPP network of charter schools. When he started his first school in the South Bronx, he believed that parental support was essential to its success. When many families pulled their kids out after just one year, he thought he was in trouble.

Some parents called him and his teaching partner, Frank Corcoran, "crazy white boys." The two had recruited forty-six fifth graders, barely enough to start the school. Twelve failed to return for sixth grade. Test scores were somewhat better than at other local schools, but Levin's discipline methods weren't working. By March of his second year he believed he had no choice but to close.

That was 1997. Thirteen years later, the academy, saved by Levin's last-minute change of mind, is a model for the ninety-nine KIPP schools in twenty states and Washington, D.C. KIPP teachers have produced the largest achievement gains for impoverished children ever seen in a single school network. Levin did it at his first school despite very mixed opening reviews from parents. The story of his school and others like it suggests that the importance of parental involvement, at least in the most disadvantaged neighborhoods, has been exaggerated. This may be because middle-class commentators have been imposing their suburban experiences on urban situations that don't match. Unchallenged, this misunderstanding of what works for low-income children could stymie efforts to produce the super schools we want.

The best school leaders I know say they don't need much parental involvement when they are hiring staff, creating class schedules, and putting discipline procedures in place. Susan Schaeffler, the founder of the cluster of KIPP schools in Washington, D.C., had no track record and little support when she and her staff started teaching fifth grade in an Anacostia church basement. She recruited students by standing in front of markets and shouting, "See me if you are interested in a school that will keep your child from eight in the morning to five in the afternoon!" That promise of free child care, in a community where most regular public schools closed at 3 p.m., persuaded some parents to give her a try. Much time passed before she was able to prove that her teachers could provide superior education as well as a longer school day.

Jaime Escalante had to extort parental action with a telephone voice that made him sound like the village priest back in Mexico. If a student missed two days of his math class, he would call the parents and threaten to notify the immigration authorities or say whatever else he thought might motivate them. Parents felt about this treatment just about the way you might expect. Only years later, after the film *Stand and Deliver* made him famous, did parents decide that Escalante could do no wrong.

This is not to say that parental involvement is a completely insignificant factor in success. Low-income parents may often be distracted just trying to make a living, but they know what works in a classroom. Once they see a school making a special effort with their children, they provide the kind of support found in suburban schools. But good schooling must come before parental support, not the other way around.

In 2006, when Sharron Hall enrolled three sons in KIPP's KEY Academy in southeast Washington, she wasn't sure it was the right move. At first she found it difficult to attend meetings the teachers called when her fifth grader, Jaquan, failed to complete his homework. The school was on a commercial strip where parking was scarce. But after three years as a KIPP parent, she was backing every move the teachers made. She was particularly pleased when they decided to have Jaquan, younger than most of his classmates, repeat sixth grade. Years before, when she'd asked another charter school to hold back a daughter who couldn't subtract 32 from 58, the teachers had laughed off the request.

Dave Levin says he has always listened to parents. But it wasn't his conversations with them that won them over. It was what they found at the school. He hired veteran teachers to help him improve discipline and start an all-school orchestra. Each year, test scores improved, until the KIPP Academy became the highest-performing middle school in the Bronx, even though its student body was 86 percent low-income.

Levin saw how strongly parents felt about the academy when administrators and parents from P.S. 31, the regular school housed in the same building, petitioned the local school board to move KIPP elsewhere. When the board convened, only a handful of P.S. 31 supporters showed up, but more than two hundred KIPP parents were there to cheer for their children's school. When the agenda item was announced, the crowd began to chant, "KIPP, KIPP, KIPP!" The district superintendent pleaded for quiet, but the chanting continued until Levin took the microphone. He thanked everyone for coming and said how pleased he was to see parents so involved. The meeting soon ended. KIPP's expulsion was no longer an issue.

Such moments have led Levin and many other principals to conclude that they should both listen to parents and do what they know is best, confident that when children succeed, their gratified families will be with them all the way.

• • •

If the secret to making a super school isn't turning it into a charter or giving parents the power to decide its leadership and staff, what must we do to create the schools we want?

How about spending more money on them? That is the favorite solution of political candidates, blue-ribbon committees, teachers' unions, and judges overseeing inequitable school funding suits. A federal judge, for instance, ordered Kansas City and the State of Missouri to sharply increase spending on the city's low-performing schools. The annual school budget jumped from $125 million in 1985 to $432 million in 1992. But it didn't work. A massive injection of extra money, without much thought or experience in using more funds, almost never works.

University of California at Berkeley professor W. Norton Grubb explains why in his book *The Money Myth: School Resources, Outcomes, and Equity* (New York: Russell Sage Foundation, 2009). He offers a list of approaches that longitudinal student achievement data suggest will work, without a large infusion of cash. For high schools, he says, the best way to go is to replace vocational and general course tracks with more demanding courses that focus on college, replace drill-filled remedial efforts with methods enriched with projects and problem-solving, provide more counseling, and raise expectations for all students.

Some of those measures I believe would work, if applied by great teachers. But I think the best guide to making a super school is not a plan of what might be done but an analysis of what has already been done. I know two instances where educators established all the essentials of a super school and succeeded. They define my vision of what all schools need to do.

The first example is the aforementioned Jaime Escalante and his math program at Garfield High. His success did not extend to the entire school. By 1987, Garfield led the country in raising math achievement for low-income Hispanics. But that program affected only about 20 percent of the students in a school with enrollment around 3,500. Still, what he did for that group was extraordinary. It was based on four methods: having high expectations for all students, creating more time for learning, using standardized tests as benchmarks of progress, and creating a team spirit.

The expectations part was easy for Escalante. He was a successful science teacher in La Paz, Bolivia, before he moved to the United States. He did not think Latino children were too fragile or too disadvantaged to learn calculus. Their only handicap was one he felt they shared with all teenagers: They were lazy. His cure for that was the second reason for his success—his skill at expanding the time they had to learn.

Escalante tried to teach not only calculus but some of the lower-level subjects, such as algebra, so he could accustom new students to his demands. If someone was struggling in any of his classes, he would wave three fingers in the student's face, a signal that the person was to report to Escalante's classroom at 3 p.m. when the final bell rang, and spend three hours doing homework. He held special Saturday classes, particularly when the AP exam neared. He persuaded the local community college to let him create summer courses that would cover geometry or trigonometry so students who started the math track late would be ready for calculus in their senior year.

The third key to his success, use of standardized tests, was controversial, but he stuck with it. He made fun of people who complained that he was teaching to the test. With an exam as deep and varied as AP Calculus AB, that was exactly what he ought to be doing, he said. He had to rid his class of the standard high school dynamic, kids versus teacher. In ordinary classrooms the students would try to persuade the teacher to ease up, maybe by not assigning so many homework questions, or by going easy on word problems. Teachers often succumbed to such pressure, at least marginally. Many teachers didn't want to give out too many bad grades or the parents would complain to the principal.

AP was different, Escalante said. If a parent complained about a low grade, he would say he was sorry, but he had to prepare his students for a three-hour exam he had not written and would not be allowed to grade. If he was too easy on his students they would not be ready for the exam. When the scores became public, if they were low, he would be blamed.

So instead he made the exams the focus of a team effort, students and teacher banding together to beat AP. There were Calculus Team shirts, hats, and bumper stickers. He told his students the calculus AP exam was the academic equivalent of the big football game each year against Roosevelt High. All his students needed to do well, he said, was hard work and *ganas*, his favorite inspirational Spanish term, which he translated as the urge to succeed.

The second example of super school creation that I personally witnessed first came to my attention in 2001, two decades after I met Escalante. I was back in Washington, D.C., having achieved my dream of being a local education reporter for the *Post*. I had heard that a new charter school was opening in one of the city's poorest neighborhoods. The day I found it, the new principal, Susan Schaeffler, was there with her father assembling chairs and desks. She was a former D.C. public school teacher who had been recruited by Mike Feinberg and Dave Levin, the KIPP founders, to start a new school in Washington. It was one of the first KIPP expansion schools launched with the support of Gap clothing empire founders Doris and Don Fisher.

Schaeffler explained to me that the school, like Feinberg's school in Houston and Levin's in the South Bronx, would be a middle school, grades five through eight. She was starting with eighty-five fifth graders, but she was not going to call them that. They would be referred to as the Class of 2009. Her father said, "I get it. That's the year they are graduating from high school."

"No, Dad," she said. "That is the year they are all going to college."

It was extraordinary, I thought, for this young teacher with no previous experience as a school administrator to think she was going to get ready for college eighty-five students whose parents had no college background. Schaeffler showed me one of the KIPP motivational devices, a weekly "paycheck" on which students were credited with a certain number of KIPP dollars, redeemable at the school store, for doing their homework, performing well in class, and not misbehaving. On the paycheck I saw a box marked "Ganas Points." She explained that this was for students who did something extra that deserved special recognition, and more KIPP dollars.

"Do you know what *ganas* means?" she asked. I said I did.

Schaeffler proceeded to build one of the most successful KIPP clusters in the country. By 2010 she had seven schools, all of them achieving far above the average for D.C. public schools. In many cases they had higher average test scores for their low-income students than affluent public schools in northwest Washington had for their middle-class students.

I began a series of interviews with Levin and Feinberg. I explored the beginnings of KIPP in my 2009 book, *Work Hard. Be Nice: How Two Inspired Teachers Created the Most Promising Schools in America*. During my five years of research for that book, I compiled a list of the essential elements of KIPP, its version of how to make a super school. That list turned out to be very similar to the one I had developed for Escalante's math program at Garfield.

The first element of success at KIPP, as well as at Garfield, was high expectations for all students. Schaeffler had said she expected all of her students to go to college. (So far, in 2010, more than 80 percent of her first class of fifth graders in 2001 have done so.)

Next was expanded learning time, about which KIPP was even more aggressive than Escalante. The Garfield teacher had to coax his worst students to stay after school and work on their lessons. At KIPP, essentially everyone stayed after school. The KIPP school day had been increased from the normal six hours to at least nine hours, 8 a.m. to 5 p.m. KIPP students were also told to attend Saturday morning classes every other week or so. A three-week summer school was part of the school year, required for everyone.

Like Jaime Escalante, KIPP teachers took standardized testing seriously. Most KIPP schools at the beginning were middle schools, so there were no Advanced Placement courses as there were at Garfield, but KIPP used standardized tests such as the Stanford 10 to gauge its progress internally and had its students take the annual state tests, as was required for all public school students. KIPP gave a nationally standardized test to all fifth graders shortly after they arrived to see how far below grade level they were. In the spring the school administered standardized tests to all grades to check their progress.

This eventually produced a testing statistic that was as startling, and as important, to me as the discovery that 26 percent of all successful Mexican-American AP calculus students in 1987 attended Garfield. In 2008, KIPP assessed the first 1,000 students who had completed all four grades of a KIPP middle school. Students from about twenty KIPP schools were involved in this assessment. Eighty percent of the students sampled had family incomes low enough to qualify for federal lunch subsidies. Ninety-five percent were black or Hispanic. On average, they had gone from the 32nd to the 60th percentile in reading and from the 40th to the 82nd percentile in math.

This was astonishing. These students had risen in just four years from typical urban levels of achievement, two or three years below grade level, to typical suburban levels, at or above grade level. I spent many months checking data on previous efforts to raise the learning level of students with those impoverished backgrounds. Gains that great for that many low-income children in one program had never happened before.

So KIPP, like Escalante, emphasized high expectations, more time for learning, and testing. The last element of the Garfield program was creating a team spirit. KIPP made that the central point of its schools' cultures. Teachers reminded students that their school was a team, and a family. They were pledged to help one another in every way. One of the worst things a KIPP student could do was to taunt or harass another student. Teachers leapt to stop such behavior immediately. The idea was that KIPP would be one place where students would not have to worry about being bullied or ridiculed, as often happened in their neighborhood schools. They could relax and focus on learning.

KIPP had a written list of principles, the Five Pillars, of which four were identical to those I had used to describe what Escalante had done. The fifth KIPP rule for building a super school was one I had not included on the Garfield list. KIPP called it "the Power to Lead." It meant that KIPP success depended on having great principals who had authority to run their schools as they thought was best for their students. KIPP schools began with the selection and training of the principal, the most important job of the KIPP national office, with the final candidates having to undergo several interviews, including some with Feinberg and Levin.

Standards were high. Sometimes KIPP officials would delay opening a school if they could not find a school leader who showed the teaching ability, love of children, people skills, and toughness they thought was necessary. The selected principals would spend a year learning administrative and financial methods, often at a business school, and then work as interns at other KIPP schools to see how successful principals did their jobs. A new KIPP principal would also often have to submit a school plan to the chartering board of whatever city the school would be located in, and begin recruiting the school's staff and students.

I had not included the leadership factor in my assessment of Garfield's strengths because of what happened after Henry Gradillas, the talented Garfield principal who served from 1982 to 1989, left to get his doctorate at Brigham Young University. Gradillas had been exactly the kind of leader a super school needed. But I noticed that the Garfield AP program remained strong, and grew even stronger, despite a series of mediocre principals who followed Gradillas. The AP math program suffered when Escalante and Jimenez left in the early 1990s, but the rest of the AP program prospered, mostly because a significant number of former Garfield students from the Escalante era went to college, got their teaching credentials, and joined the faculty at their old school.

I have learned enough in the years since to conclude that Garfield's success despite a lack of leadership was a fluke. Super schools need super principals. KIPP has shown that a school cannot reach the necessary level of success, at least in inner-city neighborhoods, unless the school leader has been an effective teacher and can identify other effective teachers.

That leader must also have the power to hire and fire teachers without interference from unions or headquarters rules. At KIPP schools, even the best principals sometimes discover someone they have hired is unable to keep to KIPP's standards. Such teachers are given a great deal of help, but if they don't improve they are dismissed, sometimes as early as Thanksgiving. The standard probation system, giving teachers two or three years to prove themselves, makes no sense to KIPP leaders. They cannot tolerate leaving their students in the hands of a substandard teacher that long. A vacancy in November is hard to fill, but KIPP officials say they have found it better to have the school's vice principal fill in, or to get a long-term substitute with special skills, rather than leave in the classroom a teacher who cannot do the job.

Many of the most important elements of creating a super school run counter to policies most districts follow. Firing a new teacher after only four months in the classroom, except in cases of abuse or criminal conduct, is unheard of. Extending the school day beyond six hours is very rare. Many school administrators, influenced by education school professors who dislike standardized testing, execute the rules for assessing school progress with tests without much enthusiasm. A school that embraces testing is often labeled a place for drilling students, filling their heads with memorized facts, and showing them that nothing in the learning process has much fun or joy.

Go on the Internet. Look for references to the "No Excuses" schools, a label applied to schools in charter networks such as KIPP, Uncommon Schools, Achievement First, YES, Aspire, Green Dot, Noble Street, and IDEA. Many of the comments will be critical. Such schools are often called militaristic and insensitive to children's needs.

Then visit some of those schools. The reality is quite different. They are strict about some things. Students must pay attention in class. They usually walk in lines when they move from one classroom to another, at least in elementary and middle school. But the atmosphere in the classes is electric. Students all participate in the lesson. There are games and songs and chants and a great deal of movement.

The long day and extended school year mean that the teachers can get a very good sense of each child's weaknesses, and discuss each child's progress every day. There is time for art and music, science and history. There is time for projects and experiments. There is time for special help for children struggling to advance, particularly those who have not mastered reading. There is time for weeklong field trips to other parts of the country, such as Washington, D.C. Students prepare for weeks for these trips and often know more than their guides about what they are seeing.

A school is not super just because it has superior test scores. It must be exciting and involving. Students must want to come to school and do the hard work it takes to learn. That requires teachers who know how to inject joy and suspense into lessons. It takes teachers who enjoy working together, and instinctively back each other up.

Schools begin not with parents, or organizational schemes, or academic theories, or special lessons, or new buildings. They begin with teachers. Get enough good ones together under the leadership of a teacher who understands all the ingredients of learning, and something very good—I won't call it quite a miracle—happens. We have enough super schools now to be sure of that. But we need many more.

PART VI

DAISY

INTRODUCTION

Daisy's Story

Daisy is a fifth grader in East Los Angeles. She works hard and is determined to go to college. She already knows where she wants to go and has written to the college, asking that she be accepted. Her dream is to be a doctor, but Daisy is about to enter one of the worst-performing schools in Los Angeles. In her neighborhood, six out of ten students don't graduate high school.

No one in Daisy's family has completed high school either. Her mother and father both dropped out to support their parents. Daisy's parents do everything they can to support their daughter because they want her to defy the odds and graduate, but private school isn't an option. Daisy's father was recently laid off and her mother is a janitor at a nearby hospital.

They have limited options, but right down the street from their home is one of the best charter schools in Los Angeles: KIPP LA Prep. Daisy has applied there with the hope of graduating high school and fulfilling her dream of becoming a doctor. KIPP's students rank among the best in Los Angeles and its demanding program will prepare Daisy for college in ways that her neighborhood public school cannot. But with 135 applicants for 10 spots, Daisy has only a 7 percent chance of getting in. . . .

Bringing Change to Scale: The Next Big Reform Challenge

Geoffrey Canada

In his more than twenty-five years with the Harlem Children's Zone, Geoffrey Canada has become nationally recognized for his pioneering work helping children and families in Harlem as well as for being a passionate advocate for education reform.

Since 1990, Canada has been the president and chief executive officer for Harlem Children's Zone, which the *New York Times Magazine* called "one of the most ambitious social-service experiments of our time."

In 1997, the agency launched the Harlem Children's Zone Project, which targets a specific geographic area in Central Harlem with a comprehensive range of services. The Zone today covers almost one hundred blocks and serves more than 8,000 children. Using the Children's Zone as a model, President Barack Obama has called for the creation of twenty "Promise Neighborhoods" across the country.

Canada grew up in the South Bronx in a poor, sometimes violent neighborhood. Despite his troubled surroundings, he was able to succeed academically, receiving a bachelor of arts degree from Bowdoin College and a master's degree in education from the Harvard School of Education.

Drawing upon his own childhood experiences and those at the Harlem Children's Zone, Canada has written two books: *Fist Stick Knife Gun: A Personal History of Violence in America* (Boston: Beacon Press, 1996) and *Reaching Up for Manhood: Transforming the Lives of Boys in America* (Boston: Beacon Press, 1998).

I am more hopeful than ever that America will break the cycle of generational poverty for millions of poor children, because we are on the verge of transforming our public education system. I have seen great schools, terrific after-school programs, and individual success stories in poor communities across America, so we know what to do—that's not the problem. The challenge is to bring these successes to scale—to change the odds for all of our kids, not just a few lucky ones.

The fact is, we don't have the luxury of ignoring this challenge. The education crisis in the United States is becoming a crisis for our entire economy, endangering our country's ability to compete in the global marketplace.

Yes, it will be hard to do. But that is no excuse for giving up. We are losing kids by the hundreds of thousands, so we have to save them in the same numbers.

We have had great successes at the Harlem Children's Zone, but we didn't do this overnight. We created a ten-year growth plan and we worked hard every year to make sure we stayed on target each step of the way. We made sure we gave every child every opportunity for success, and we absolutely refused to give up on even the toughest cases. In fact, we went out of our way to recruit them. We treated this like the life-or-death situation it is for our kids. We worked weekends and holidays, and if one of my staff produced excuses instead of results, he or she was out of a job. It was our responsibility to make sure our children succeeded and would do whatever it took to make that happen. I wanted to prove what a whole neighborhood of poor children could do if the playing field was level.

We very intentionally created footprints other communities could follow, since the problems in Harlem were the same as those in many urban areas where you can predict how kids will do simply by looking at their zip code.

Nationally, we have more than 1 million students dropping out of high school. For black teenagers, the high school graduation rate is less than 50 percent. But those kinds of statistics are only the beginning of the tragic story in poor minority neighborhoods. I recently saw a police department list of the gangs operating in Harlem. Some of the gang names were revealing: Cash Money Brothers, Addicted to Green, The Get Money Boys. For a young man with few job skills, drug dealing and running with gangs may seem like the only real option for earning a living. Sixty percent of young black men who drop out of school land in prison by their thirties—and incarceration costs can run more than $40,000 a year. These young people end up paying no taxes, and they don't make a positive contribution to society.

The entire country is paying the price for this failure. Can we afford to scale up the kinds of educational programs that work? I'd turn the question around and ask, can we afford *not* to? If America is to continue to be a preeminent force in the world and sustain our economic viability, we can't afford a status quo that shuttles hundreds of thousands of our children toward prison instead of the job market.

The educational outlook for children who are trapped in devastated neighborhoods has been dismal since I was attending P.S. 99 in the South Bronx back in the 1960s, but I believe our country is finally on the verge of systemic change.

Americans sometimes forget that we have many great public schools that are already meeting their stated goal—to educate children at a very high level so they can go on to postsecondary education and successful careers. Some of these effective public schools are in affluent suburbs and wealthy city neighborhoods, but many others are in low- or middle-income communities where teachers, administrators, and families have banded together to implement programs that work for the benefit of students. So the country has *already* scaled successful education practices in every state and practically every city.

However, when we look at the children who are still failing—many of them poor and, in particular, children of color—we see an array of challenges that have to be tackled simultaneously. But if we are going to be serious about changing the trajectories for large numbers of children in poor communities, we have to reform the current public school system. We can look at great charter schools for inspiration, but the traditional public school system is what ultimately needs to be changed for us to change the horrific status quo we have been living with in America.

Innovation is one of the keys to the reform we need, and one of the major reasons why charter schools will play an important role in the years to come. Many of today's failing traditional public schools have been failing for decades and are tragically following the same strategies year after year to no avail. A well-run charter school, on the other hand, will not lock itself into a strategy that is ineffective. Because of the greater administrative and regulatory freedom at charter schools, successful ones have been able to suspend many of the public school practices that inhibit innovation and experiment with new approaches that are more effective.

Of course, having a different strategy doesn't guarantee success. Some charter schools have proved to be as bad as the public schools they were created to replace—or even worse. However, opponents of charter schools have tried to use these failures to suggest that the entire charter school movement is a failure and should be discontinued or severely scaled back. There is not a lot of logic in this argument.

To ignore the successful charter schools and what they have been able to do because some other charter schools *don't* work flies in the face of the logic of why charter schools were created. The idea behind charter schools was that a group of individuals would be given enough flexibility to create an innovative strategy. If the strategy fails and the school is unable to correct it, the chartering entity (which may be the state board of education, the local school district, or another government agency) has the right to close that school. And I would argue that they should exercise that right with all deliberate speed. But if the strategy succeeds, then other schools should study it, learn from it, and emulate it.

So from the beginning, the charter school movement has been about innovation and experimentation. Any scientist will tell you that not all experiments succeed. The point is to learn from the ones that do, and to spread the benefits as quickly and widely as possible. That some charter experiments have failed shouldn't be used to short-circuit the entire process.

Today the charter school movement has a long enough track record that we can begin to ask, and answer, the crucial question: What makes a great charter school? There are several factors, and they point toward some of the reforms we need to transform the larger traditional public school system, which would address the "scale" problem and help millions of children.

All of us who have run schools realize that a great leader is one of the most important elements in a school's success. A leader's ability to hire, inspire, train, and, where necessary, remove instructors directly correlates to that school's success. Charter school governing boards, which have the ultimate responsibility for selecting and supporting school administrators, principals, and other leaders, need to take that responsibility very seriously. Politics has to be put aside when we select a school leader; competence, effectiveness, vision, and energy should be the criteria. And when the results fall short, the board shouldn't hesitate to change the leadership. Accountability begins at the top, in a great school as in any other organization.

Another key ingredient is hiring teachers and staff who are well trained and—like the top leadership—hold themselves accountable for the success of their students. When students aren't successful and their teacher begins to talk about the problems with the community, the family, the siblings, or the larger society before looking at what may have been wrong with his or her efforts in the classroom, you have the wrong teacher. Finding great teachers is the "secret sauce" of great schools and, in particular, great charter schools.

And if a school is to be staffed with great teachers, it must have the ability to retain and reward excellence. Teachers who understand that their value is acknowledged through compensation—both monetary and symbolic—recognize that they are part of a system whose leadership is focused on the end goal of student success. By contrast, where teachers work hard and deliver results but are not appreciated and rewarded, they become dispirited and will inevitably leave the school or drop out of the profession altogether.

At the Harlem Children's Zone Promise Academy charter schools, our teachers get bonuses based on how well students have been doing in their classroom. Since we test our kids regularly to help guide our instruction, we are also able to track how well our teachers are doing. And because teaching is such incredibly hard work, we also show our appreciation by paying for teachers to have some fun, such as a night out at a Broadway show or a baseball game.

Another bonus we give to teachers is regular exposure to top-quality professional development, since great teachers are always excited about learning new ways they can help their students. Naturally, this benefits the students as well—a great example of having incentives aligned so that everyone emerges a winner.

Many successful charter schools share other innovative practices that offer additional advantages to students. For example, a longer school day and a longer school year are essential for helping children from communities with high rates of failure. (The average school year in the United States is just 180 days, as compared with 190 days in New Zealand, 200 in the Netherlands, 220 in South Korea, and 243 in Japan.) In an effort to provide students with enough time on task to make up areas in which they are deficient, many charter schools (including ours) are run during the summer, weekends, and the holidays when other schools are closed.

An additional key component of charter schools is accountability and the use of data to measure student performance and to drive improvement. Smart leaders at many charter schools are rejecting the common system of relying solely on high-stakes statewide tests of student achievement. The test results come back so late in the school year that it is nearly impossible to use them to shape and improve instruction during the school year in which they are given.

Instead, at successful schools there is a constant focus on getting real information about students' performance early and often, using that data to have a much more granular look at a student's ability, then creating an action plan to target an individual student's deficiencies. These data are also used to determine whether overall educational strategies are working. The ability to collect, use, and interpret data in an ongoing way is something at which many successful charter schools excel—and something that public schools can certainly learn to do as well.

Finally, we need to recognize the powerful impact that forces outside the schools have on students' achievement. Sometimes the effort to improve students' outcomes gets hung up in a debate about whether to focus solely on schools or to target the factors around schools, such as families and neighborhood conditions.

I believe that the only way to do what is really necessary to change the odds for the hundreds of thousands of poor children in this country is to tackle both. We need to improve schools at the same time we address the barriers to academic success outside schools—from health problems to misguided parenting practices to lack of physical safety.

We need to broaden our definition of education—to see it as a process that starts before kindergarten and takes place outside of school as well as inside. Particularly in communities that historically have struggled with academic performance, we need to begin our efforts at birth and to make sure all of our children are on track by the time they enter kindergarten. In these troubled neighborhoods, we should ensure that children's critical needs are addressed as a matter of course.

For example, we know that when a child misses school repeatedly due to a chronic condition, such as asthma, a medical problem becomes an education problem. At the Harlem Children's Zone, we decided to tackle the issue head-on. In partnership with Harlem Hospital, we conducted a survey of children in the neighborhood and found that more than 30 percent had asthma—several times the national rate. Working with the hospital, we created a program to educate families about managing the disease, even sending staff into homes looking for asthma triggers (such as mold, allergens from pets, or secondhand smoke) and helping parents eliminate them. By teaching families how to be proactive in controlling the disease, they cut down on emergency-room visits and significantly reduced the number of school days the children missed because of asthma.

Another key to running a successful school is the coordination of after-school services and supports. After-school time offers an opportunity to target individual students' needs and reinforce lessons, as well as to engage in wonderfully appropriate youth development activities focused on culture, arts, and recreation. A good after-school program can address the needs of the entire child—physical, mental, and intellectual—by providing a safe, enriching environment that is a far better alternative to hanging out on the streets. In the Harlem Children's Zone after-school programs, hundreds of teenagers are introduced to fun, enriching activities, from karate to video production to fashion design. But we also make sure they all get tutoring, and we have academic case managers monitoring each student's school progress. There's no conflict between academic achievement and recreation—in fact, they can and should reinforce each other.

All of the systemic innovations I've just described could easily be applied to our public school systems if the will to do so were present.

I believe the key to bringing educational reform to scale is allowing competition to thrive in this area of American society that has been organized so as to discourage competition. The people who found and run charter schools aren't any smarter or more dedicated than the majority of American educators. The big difference is that they are able to experiment. The good charter schools hopefully will survive and grow, while the bad ones will go out of business. That is exactly the kind of competition that public education in America needs.

There are already public schools that mimic the best practices of successful charter schools. But they often do so without the permission or blessing of school leadership entities—school boards, superintendents, and unions. One of the reasons our country needs to continue supporting charter schools is that the current mainstream educational structure makes it almost impossible for traditional public schools to innovate and change.

Teachers unions have done a good job of representing educators as employees and defending their rights. But one of the by-products of the strong teachers' unions in this country is that teacher contracts define with excessive specificity what a teacher can and cannot do in the classroom. And once you define everything that can happen in a school—how many hours teachers work, how many classes they teach, how long their lunch breaks and bathroom breaks are, and the details of their compensation structures—you deprive the leader, the principal, the director, and even the teachers themselves of the ability to try new things, thereby strangling any hope of innovation. So the more successful the unions have been in defining everything that teachers may do, the less able a principal or leader is to bring change to the system—even when that system has chronically failed the kids.

Unfortunately, efforts to allow innovation and creativity to flourish have too often been seen as anti-union. I am not suggesting that unions alone are the problem, nor would I claim that simply eliminating unions will make our schools better all by itself. There are many failing schools in communities that don't have teachers' unions. But I am suggesting that where unions are too strong, the principals have very little ability to introduce the kinds of innovations that have made charter schools into trailblazers for educational reform.

Consider, for example, the simple matter of the number of hours in the school day and days in the school year. If a child is two years behind in reading and math, shouldn't he or she get the opportunity to stay in school for a longer day to catch up with the other students? Shouldn't a student who is failing be able to work through the summer to master the skills the other kids have already learned? In most rationally run businesses, employees have to work late when they fall behind, but you can't do that in public education.

Then there's the issue of how employees are evaluated, compensated, and retained. In ordinary businesses, employees who are unable or unwilling to perform their duties are terminated. Not so in public education, where union contracts establish convoluted procedures for eliminating even the most incompetent teachers. Teachers' unions often oppose even the gathering of data that could help determine teacher effectiveness.

I am not saying that teachers' unions don't want children to be successful. I believe that they do. But they are very good at protecting the rights of the adults they represent; in fact, they protect those rights so well that the rights of the children to get a good education have sometimes been subordinated to the rights of the adults. That has to change. Poor kids—who have so many things working against their success—can't afford a lousy teacher. I believe that the needs of children should trump the job security of the small number of teachers who should not be in a classroom.

On the other hand, we need to really rethink how we pay teachers so we attract and keep the best and brightest. American teachers are woefully underpaid. Starting salaries should be in the $50,000–$60,000 range, at a minimum, to attract the kind of talent we need in education. Teachers should be paid like full-time employees, not part-time employees—but they should be required to work a full-time job.

Incentives for performance should also be introduced, so an extraordinary teacher will be rewarded the same way employees are rewarded for extraordinary performance in business or law or medicine. There is nothing revolutionary or subversive about rewarding teachers based on merit.

This, then, is the basic formula for bringing educational reform to scale across America: Create the right incentive structures, remove the obstacles to children's achievement, give kids the social and academic supports they need, encourage smart experimentation, and use data to drive results.

It's the children who go to school, but how they do is the responsibility of the adults around them—all of us. The success of *all* of America's children is a measure of how well we *all* are fulfilling that responsibility. I have seen what this country can do and I believe we are up to the task.

Educating America's Young People for the Global Economy

Bill and Melinda Gates

Bill Gates and Melinda French Gates are cochairs of the Bill & Melinda Gates Foundation, along with William H. Gates Sr. They shape and approve grantmaking strategies, advocate for the foundation's issues, and help set the overall direction of the organization. They also participate in national and international events and travel extensively to focus attention on the issues the foundation champions.

Bill Gates cofounded Microsoft Corp. in 1975 with his childhood friend Paul Allen. He still serves as its chairman. Melinda Gates joined Microsoft in 1987, leading the development of many of its multimedia products. In 1996, she retired from her position as Microsoft's general manager of information products. The Gateses live in Medina, Washington, with their three children.

It's easy when talking about education reform to get lost in the statistics: the dropout rates, the test scores, and the spending figures. Certainly numbers make problems quantifiable, and they help us to see where systems break down and how they might be fixed.

But while statistics help us define the need for reform, it's the people—the students, the teachers, and the principals—who make those numbers real. It's too easy to forget that education reform isn't about jobs, or policy, or statistics. It's about real people.

We have had the privilege of visiting many schools over the past decade and learning about the challenges they face. Melinda often reflects on her experience of meeting a young woman at a public high school in south Los Angeles. She was preparing to become a manicurist in a salon. That's a fine choice—if it's a real choice. But for her, it wasn't. She had no option to go on to college if she wanted to. She was locked in a course of study that—even if she aced it—would not prepare her for any postsecondary studies. In one of her math classes, she was learning to read the back of a can of soup.

We have met many young people on this same path. They graduate from high school without ever knowing how far behind they are. They get a job, but they cannot survive on the income, so they enroll at a community college part-time. They have to take remedial math and English. But college is expensive, they don't earn college credit for remedial classes, and the classes aren't offered at times that fit their work schedule. So they drop out. Many factors are to blame, but the biggest reason is that their education did not prepare them to earn a degree beyond high school. They were never given the opportunity to do what it takes to improve their lives.

This is why we've made improving America's education system a priority for our foundation.

We've taken on some tough issues: eradicating malaria, developing disease-resistant seed for farmers in the developing world, and combating family homelessness in the Pacific Northwest. But we often say to each other that, out of everything our foundation does, improving education in America may be the toughest challenge we've taken on.

We created our foundation with the belief that all people—regardless of background, circumstance, or geography—should have the chance to lead healthy and productive lives. In the United States, we chose to focus on education because it is the surest path to opportunity. Achieving that opportunity should be within reach for hundreds of thousands more young people in this country.

The students, parents, teachers, innovators, and community leaders whom we have met during the past ten years give us great optimism that we are all on the cusp of deep and lasting improvement in our public schools.

For much of America's history, its public schools were the subject of great civic pride. They were the cornerstone of our fundamental belief that through hard work and opportunity, young people could become anything they wanted to be. Our high schools were established generations ago when good-paying factory jobs were plentiful. We prepared only a fraction of students for college because for most Americans, college wasn't necessary to earn a wage that would let them support a family.[1]

But those days are gone. The global economy now is primarily based on knowledge and technology. Critical thinking and problem-solving skills are paramount, as are the abilities to innovate and to collaborate with others.

These are the traits today's employers value in their workers. We both know this firsthand from our experiences at Microsoft. Companies like Microsoft increasingly need highly skilled and well-educated workers in order to remain strong and grow. America must ensure that our young people are well positioned for these jobs.

But despite the best efforts of many committed educators, our high schools have not adapted. Classes are still separated into forty-minute chunks; the learning day ends at 3 p.m.; schools shut down for a long summer vacation—all vestiges of our agrarian and industrial past.

It goes deeper. Many schools do not have the data to tell us how a student is or is not progressing and why. We do not have clear, consistent standards across states that are based on the evidence of what colleges and employers need. And in most schools there is little room for taking a new approach to education.

As a result, many students end up bored and disengaged from their high school curriculum.[2] They're native to a digital age, but they're shoehorned into an archaic learning model. The results are devastating.

Today, nearly a third of our students fail to graduate from high school with their class.[3] For those who do graduate and make it to a community college, roughly 60 percent will need to take at least one remedial class.[4] For low-income students or those of color, the deck is stacked high against them. Only about 19 percent of Hispanics between the ages of twenty-five and thirty-four earn a degree from a two-year or four-year school. For African Americans, it's 29 percent.[5]

Those numbers simply aren't good enough for a strong America and a vibrant, competitive economy. A recent report from the Center on Education and the Workforce at Georgetown University shows why.

The report, *Help Wanted: Projections of Jobs and Education Requirements Through 2018*, forecasted that over the next eight years, 63 percent of all American jobs will require some sort of postsecondary education. What's more, American employers will need nearly 22 million new workers with postsecondary degrees. But the center's research shows that our higher education system will fall short of that mark by 3 million graduates.[6]

That's a pretty compelling argument for why we need an improved education system in the United States. It also affirms the importance of our foundation's recent work with higher education institutions, where we and our partners are working to dramatically increase college graduation rates.

Although we have one of the lowest high school graduation rates in the industrialized world,[7] America nevertheless excels at sending many of those students who do graduate high school to college—since 1980, enrollments at postsecondary institutions have increased by more than half.[8] Unfortunately, only about half of those college students will earn a degree. For minority and low-income students the graduation rates are much, much worse.[9]

And so as our foundation has gotten deeper into our postsecondary work over the past two years, it's become increasingly clear that even those students who make it through high school with decent grades still are not prepared for college-level work. Even when we set our sights on colleges and universities, we still end up at the original problem: high school.

Our foundation has been working for nearly a decade to improve high school graduation rates and college readiness. When we started, we were primarily focused on making schools smaller. We hoped that if we could make schools more personalized and engaging, we could drive down dropout rates and increase student achievement. The results of that early effort were mixed, and at the same time highly enlightening.

Some of the schools we worked with made strong gains, but many of the schools that were involved in our initial focus never showed much improvement.[10] When we examined why that was, we saw that successful schools made more than structural changes to the size or organization of the school. Their improvement seemed to be spurred by what was happening inside the class-room, where excellent teaching, high standards, and a strong cur-riculum took precedent.

In retrospect, it seems so simple: *Great teaching* explained the difference in student achievement among those schools. And it also explained why success was so spotty. Results that depend on great teaching can't be replicated on campuses that lack great teachers. Studies show that the impact on student learning of having an effective teacher is greater than the impact of any other factor inside a school.[11] For example, being taught for four years by a teacher in the top quarter of ability versus a teacher in the bottom quarter can help eliminate the achievement gap in test scores for African-American students.[12]

As we move forward in our education efforts, our strategy has at its heart the relationship and interactions that take place between students and teachers in the classroom. In short, we're now focused on effective teaching: identifying it, nurturing it, studying it, and replicating it. Of course, principals, parents, and others must be fully invested in the success of the education sys-tem as well.

But we realize that to be truly effective, teachers need sup-port. They need clear and consistent college-ready standards to which they can teach. They need constructive, meaningful feed-back and opportunities to grow and improve. They need infor-mation and data on their students' strengths and weaknesses. And they need to be part of the process to create those systems along the way.

How do you set up a system so that every teacher has access to each of these things?

We're supporting groundbreaking research in partnership with schools, teachers' unions, and communities across the country to answer this basic question. We're also on a quest to discover what makes an effective teacher. What can we do to put an effective teacher in every classroom, every year?

To achieve this, we must understand what makes an effective teacher. We know which teachers produce great student outcomes based on standardized tests, but we do not know the specific ingredients that make these teachers great.

To find out, we launched Intensive Partnerships for Effective Teaching in the fall of 2009 to support bold local plans to study and transform how teachers are recruited, rewarded, and retained. Our partnerships were launched in Hillsborough County, Florida; Memphis, Tennessee; Pittsburgh, Pennsylvania; and a group of charter schools in Los Angeles called The College-Ready Promise. Schools in these districts teach more than 350,000 students, and we believe they can be national models.

We are especially optimistic because in each place all the players are working together: administrators, teachers and their unions, elected officials, community leaders, and parents.

We know that a reform will never take root and flourish if teachers don't support it. We are partnering with the American Federation of Teachers to support innovative ideas for evaluating teachers, including a pay-for-performance plan based on multiple measures of student learning. And in our Intensive Partnerships for Effective Teaching sites, educators are helping overturn decades of entrenched policies in favor of new ways to recruit, develop, assign, evaluate, retain, compensate, and promote teachers. This is truly remarkable work because so much progress has come so quickly.

At the heart of our collaboration is an effort to create fair and reliable measures of teacher effectiveness that are tied to gains in student achievement. This is a sea change because, for the most part, public schools have seldom meaningfully coupled their teacher evaluations with student achievement.

Most teachers are evaluated by an administrator only two or three times a year. Typically, school principals or their assistants will briefly drop in to a teacher's classroom to observe a lesson. Based on what the administrator sees during that twenty minutes or so, he or she will fill out a standard evaluation form, along with checking off boxes for things like "arrives on time" and "maintains professional appearance."[13]

There is very little professional feedback on or analysis of what the administrators saw, or how the teacher could be better. There is rarely an attempt to correlate the administrator's observations to how much, or how little, the students in the class learned.[14]

From our conversations with teachers and union leaders, it's clear that many educators are frustrated that they do not get the help they need to coax more from their students. In 2008 and 2009, our foundation partnered with Scholastic Inc. to conduct a national survey, and we heard from some 40,000 teachers on crucial questions facing the profession. The survey reveals that teachers overwhelmingly believe that professional development is crucial to their success and that of their students, and that they want more feedback about their performance in the classroom.[15]

We also found that they want to be rewarded for their results. And this is where things get really exciting.

Through our Measures of Effective Teaching effort, we're using technology, data, and research to help educators develop new, fair evaluations that will give teachers the feedback they crave.

But to provide that kind of feedback, you have to get into classrooms. You have to stay for more than twenty minutes. And you have to do more than check off a bunch of boxes. This project is going to emphasize classes with big achievement gains, and we'll try to puzzle out what those teachers did that was so effective.

This research will give districts the information they need to make better use of investments in public education. America spends about $8 billion a year to reward teachers who have earned master's degrees, even though some evidence says that in most cases a teacher's master's degree does nothing to improve student achievement. Our nation is spending billions funding salary schedules based on a seniority system, even though the evidence says that after the first five years, seniority does not impact student achievement. We've spent billions to reduce class size, even though there is no strong evidence that reducing class size in high school improves student performance.[16]

We need to invest in approaches and methods where there is evidence of significant student gains and achievement. The research our partners are conducting will give districts the evidence they need to create fair evaluation systems that base compensation on student achievement and pay teachers what they're worth.

We're already seeing it happen. In Pittsburgh, the school district and the teachers' union recently ratified a new contract that both sides are calling a new way of doing business. The five-year agreement includes new incentives for teachers, including a pilot program that could grant teachers up to $8,000 in extra pay a year, provided students make substantial academic gains. Teachers, administrators, and board members have all called this new contract historic.[17]

We don't think it's possible to overstate the importance of the work school districts such as Pittsburgh are taking on. They've made creating and nurturing effective teachers the center of their work.

But even this probably isn't enough. Even the most effective and successful educators need guidance on what to teach and when to teach it. Our survey with Scholastic revealed that teachers favor establishing clear and common academic standards, so that must be a priority as well.[18]

The Common Core Standards initiative, a movement led by the nation's governors and state school superintendents, has brought together parents, teachers, principals, researchers, and other education experts to develop consistent, rigorous academic standards for math and English.

We believe that high standards for all students are indispensable to high achievement. In an era when technology makes it easy to forge friendships and business partnerships around the globe, there's no reason that the academic standards in Washington state shouldn't be as high as standards in Maine or anywhere else.

Even as these standards set the bar for the skills and knowledge all young people should have when they graduate high school, they still allow for a flexible approach. Different states, different regions, and different teachers in different cultures will teach to these standards in different ways. But all students will be taught to the same high standards, wherever they were born and no matter where they go to school.

These things—measuring, defining, and nurturing effective teaching along with adopting college-ready academic standards—are critically important to ensuring that every child in every classroom is prepared for success.

Finally, our school system desperately needs innovation, particularly when it comes to bringing technology into the classroom. Charter schools are important because they have enormous latitude for innovation. Public charter schools can identify effective ways to bring technology into the classroom, and those approaches can then be replicated in traditional public schools.

For example, we've been really impressed by Rocketship Education in San Jose, California. The leaders at Rocketship divided the curriculum into two parts. The first is a critical-thinking component, which is taught by master teachers in the traditional classroom. The second is a basic-skills component, which they discovered can be taught effectively in an online learning lab.

The results have been excellent. Students at both Rocketship campuses are scoring higher on state tests than those from wealthy districts like Palo Alto, even though almost 80 percent come from low-income families, and almost that many are English language learners.[19]

This is a challenging and exciting time in education. There is definitely a convergence of ideas and opportunity around education reform and a belief that all children need and deserve an education that prepares them for the demands of college and careers. Many national and local leaders, teachers, parents, and others share a desire to dramatically improve education for all children in America regardless of their background or circumstance. Many have been working on these issues for a long time.

We are optimistic that change is within reach. But we must all advocate for what works. We must all be willing to make tough choices. Once evidence and best practices are in hand, we need to work to replicate these approaches and policies.

Parents and students everywhere want the same thing—the opportunity to learn and achieve at the highest level—and they are willing to work hard to experience it. Our challenge is to provide them with that opportunity, no matter what kind of school they attend and no matter whether they are from a poor neighborhood or a more affluent community.

When we look ahead to the next ten years, we are reminded of KIPP, a charter school in Houston where we saw great teachers in action. The results are clear: KIPP graduates more than 95 percent of its students, compared to the district average of 70 percent. Almost 90 percent of the graduates go on to a four-year college.[20] If we commit to a country where this is a reality for all young people, we'll raise the next generation of Americans to be better educated, more creative, more productive, and ready to compete at the leading edge of the knowledge economy.

That's a change that will enhance the life of every American—and it's one we're ready to help make.

PART VII

WHAT YOU CAN DO

How You Can Make a Difference*

The Alliance for Excellent Education

The Alliance for Excellent Education (www.all4ed.org) is a Washington, D.C.-based national policy and advocacy organization that works to improve national and federal policy so that all students can achieve at high academic levels and graduate from high school ready for success in college, work, and citizenship in the twenty-first century. The alliance focuses on America's 6 million most at-risk secondary school students—those in the lowest achievement quartile—who are most likely to leave school without a diploma or to graduate unprepared for a productive future.

The alliance encourages the development and implementation of federal and national policies that support effective high school reform and increased student achievement and attainment. To enlighten the national debate about education policies and options, the group works to synthesize and distribute research and information about promising practices. The alliance also provides sound, objective, nonpartisan advice that informs decisions about creating and implementing policies. Working with educators, researchers, business leaders, citizen groups, and decision makers at the local, state, and national levels, the alliance develops federal policy

*Excerpted with permission from the web site of The Alliance for Excellent Education.

recommendations and advocates to policy makers in the federal government.

To encourage public awareness and action that support effective secondary school reform, the alliance publishes many briefs, reports, and fact sheets; hosts numerous events and makes presentations—in D.C., on Capitol Hill, and around the country; issues regular press releases providing national and state-level data and information about the impact of improving educational achievement and attainment levels for secondary school students; and collaborates with policy makers, researchers, and educators to advance the organization's goals. The alliance also publishes a biweekly newsletter, *Straight A's*, which provides information on public education policy and progress in an accessible format.

The alliance's audience includes policy makers at the federal, state, and local levels; education organizations; the corporate, labor, and funding communities; the media; parents, administrators, teachers, and students; and a concerned public.

Regardless of their plans, all of the nation's young people need high-level knowledge and skills to achieve success in a rapidly changing world of technological advances and international competition. And every American has a stake in their success, regardless of whether they have school-age children of their own.

You don't have to be a school superintendent or member of Congress to help the 6 million students most at risk of failing to graduate from high school. This chapter outlines a few steps that every individual can take to help to reform America's high schools. It begins with our analysis of the ten elements of a successful high school—a kind of checklist any citizen can use to evaluate local education at the high school level—followed by suggestions for specific actions that students, parents, educators, and businesspeople can take to help improve the quality of schooling at the local, state, and national levels. It's an effort that requires everyone's support to be fully effective.

The Ten Elements of a Successful High School

How effective is your community's high school in educating its students? Drawing from the work of leading researchers and educators from around the country, The Alliance for Excellent Education has identified ten key elements that every high school should have in place to ensure that all its students are successful. The list includes challenging classes, a safe learning environment, and skilled teachers. Whether you are a parent seeking a stronger education for your child, a business owner in need of a well-trained workforce, or a concerned citizen joining with others to improve schools, this checklist can help you identify the strengths and weaknesses of your community schools and guide you in determining how you can help improve them.

Challenging Classes

All students must learn the advanced skills that are key to success in college and in the twenty-first-century workplace. Every student should take demanding classes in the core subjects of English, history, science, and math; *no student* should ever get a watered-down course of study. Further, students should also be given the opportunity to earn industry certification or some college credit while in high school through programs such as Advanced Placement, International Baccalaureate, or those offered through a local college or university.

Personal Attention for All Students

Every high school should be small enough—or divided into small enough units—to allow teachers and staff to get to know all students as individuals and to respond to their specific learning needs. By the ninth grade, students should have a detailed plan for graduation—identifying the specific courses they must take, opportunities they should pursue, and extra help they need to succeed in high school and beyond. And every student should receive frequent and ongoing support from at least one academic adviser throughout the high school years.

Extra Help for Those Who Need It

Every high school should have a system in place to identify kids as soon as they start to struggle in reading, math, or any core subject, and every school should reserve time and resources for the immediate help those kids need to stay on course.

Bringing the Real World to the Classroom

High schools should help students make the connection between book learning and the skills needed to be successful in life. Students must develop the necessary work habits, character, and sense of personal responsibility to succeed in school, at work, and in society. As part of their class work, students should have opportunities to design independent projects, conduct experiments, solve open-ended problems, and be involved in activities that connect school to the rest of the world.

Family and Community Involvement

Students thrive when their high schools encourage positive learning relationships among families, educators, faith groups, civic organizations, businesses, and other members of the community. Parents should have many chances to visit the school building, talk with teachers and staff, voice concerns, share ideas, serve as volunteers, and suggest ways to improve the school. And school leaders should reach out to their neighbors by attending community events and forming partnerships with local organizations to increase effectiveness and tap additional resources.

A Safe Learning Environment

Every high school must guarantee the safety of its students, teachers, staff, and visitors, and every school should be kept free of drugs, weapons, and gangs. School leaders should build a climate of trust and respect, encourage peaceful solutions to conflict, and respond directly to any bullying, verbal abuse, or other threats.

Skilled Teachers

Every high school teacher should know well the subjects she teaches and should know well how to teach all kinds of students, from all kinds of backgrounds. New teachers should get the guidance and mentoring they need to be successful in the classroom. All teachers should have enough time to plan lessons, carefully review student performance, and continuously improve their teaching.

Strong Leaders

Every high school needs a skillful principal, one who supervises personnel effectively, manages finances capably, and keeps the organization running smoothly. Every school also needs a strong educational leader (this could be the principal, a senior teacher, or another staff member), to define a vision of academic excellence, work with teachers to develop an engaging and coherent curriculum, and serve as a mentor and role model for teachers and students alike.

Necessary Resources

Every high school should provide all students and teachers with the books, computers, laboratory equipment, technology, and other resources they need to be successful. And every school should maintain safe, clean facilities that are fit for teaching and learning.

User-Friendly Information

All community members should have easy access to information that gives a clear, straightforward picture of how well the school is serving all of its students, including those from every income level, ethnic group, and racial background. Some of the key pieces of information include a school's graduation requirements, graduation and dropout rates, and student performance on state tests.

How Students Can Make a Difference

At the Local Level

- Tell your teachers, counselors, relatives, and friends that you want and expect to go to college. Make sure that your counselor has enrolled you in a course of study that prepares you for college. Develop a plan for graduation, college, and career with the help of your counselor, parents, guardian, and/or mentor.

- Take pictures, make a video, keep a diary, or make a list of the problems students in your high school face. Post this information on a Web site for classmates and others who may be interested.

- Talk to your parents or other family members about the problems in your high school. Ask your parents or guardian to join and seek change through the Parent Teacher Association or other local organizations dedicated to education reform.

- Write a letter to the school newspaper or local newspaper editor to share your views about how to make high schools better.

- Launch a civic engagement activity with your classmates seeking to share your views about making high schools better with the mayor, city council members, business leaders, and school administrators in your city. Ask local business leaders to sponsor a high school community forum, video showing, or student advocacy trip to the state capitol and/or Washington, D.C.

At the State Level

- Make a video of students giving testimonials about their high school experiences.

- Call or write to your state representatives and ask them to review the video and share it with their colleagues.

- Organize your friends and classmates to launch a letter-writing campaign requesting that your governor, chief state school officer, and state representatives and senators reform high schools for the better.

- Organize a group of students to take a trip to your state's capitol to schedule meetings with state legislators.

At the National Level

- Make a video of students giving testimonials about their high school experiences.

- Call or write to your Congress members and ask them to review the video and share it with their colleagues.

- Organize your friends and classmates to launch a letter-writing campaign requesting that the president and Congress reform high schools for the better.

- Organize a group of students to take a trip to Washington, D.C., to schedule meetings with congressional representatives and senators.

How Parents Can Make a Difference

At the Local Level

- Visit your state's school report card to learn more about your high school's graduation, dropout, literacy, and school safety rates and visit School Matters (www.schoolmatters.com) to compare your school to others in your area.

- If you want your child to graduate on time prepared for college, talk to your child's teacher and counselor to ensure that he or she is enrolled in a college preparatory curriculum and is on track to meet the school's graduation requirements.

- If your child's grades or teacher indicates that it is needed, make sure that he or she gets extra tutoring help after school. If your school does not provide after-school tutoring, contact your mayor's office to locate programs run by community organizations.

- Contact your school district superintendent to find out whether the district has plans to implement high school reforms. Request immediate action if no initiative is planned.

- Write an article for your local paper or community newsletter about your observations or experiences.

- Start or become active in your school's *Parent Teacher Association* to get more resources to help your child and convince local members to champion high school reform.

- Contact your local school board for a meeting schedule. Attend meetings and demand they give more attention to high school reform.

- Although your local elected officials may not have direct responsibility for your area schools, request a meeting with, call, or send a letter to your mayor and/or city council members to discuss strategies for raising community awareness about high school reform.

At the State Level

- Invite your elected officials to visit your child's high school to engage administrators, teachers, and students in a conversation about how high schools should be improved.

- Write letters to, call, and/or request a meeting with your state elected representatives to share your concerns and the need for reform.

- Contact the Public Education Network (www.public education.org) to find an advocacy organization near you focused on high school reform.

- Work with the Parent Teacher Association or another advocacy organization to develop or participate in a lobby day at the state capitol focused on high school education accountability and reform.

- Contact your state's chief school officer to request more information about plans for improving high schools.

- If there are not enough library, computer, and/or textbook resources in your child's school, ask your state legislators and chief school officer to seek more support for your high school and others like it.

At the National Level

- Invite your elected officials to visit your child's high school to engage administrators, teachers, and students in a conversation about how high schools should be improved.

- Write letters to, call, and/or request meetings with your congressional representatives to share your concerns and the need for reform.

- Contact The Alliance for Excellent Education or the Public Education Network to find a national advocacy organization focused on high school reform.

- Join with an organization to participate in a lobby day at the U.S. Capitol focused on high school education accountability and reform.

- Contact the assistant secretary for communications and outreach at the U.S. Department of Education to request more information about plans for reforming high schools.

- Ask your congressional representatives to increase federal funding for high schools.

- Visit The Alliance for Excellent Education to sign up for updates about national high school reform initiatives and congressional action alerts.

How Educators Can Make a Difference

At the Local Level

- Visit School Matters (www.schoolmatters.com) to download a report card on your state's high schools.

- Research best practices and incorporate techniques into the high school or classroom setting.

- Visit schools and districts that have adopted or are undertaking significant high school reforms.

- Pursue professional development opportunities that incorporate new thinking about high school curriculum and instruction.

- If you work in the school, connect with your district superintendent to share why high school reform is important. Request a districtwide in-service day highlighting best practices in high school reform.

At the State Level

- Contact the Parent Teacher Association or professional organizations for educators to find out whether they sponsor state lobbying initiatives. If so, attend and support the initiatives focused on educating state elected officials about the need for stronger high schools.

- If there are not enough library, computer, and/or textbook resources in your school, ask your state legislators and chief school officer to seek more support for your high school and others like it.

- Connect with an existing "P–20" Council that coordinates state education from pre-kindergarten through graduate education, or ask the governor to establish one.

At the National Level

- Contact professional organizations for educators to find out whether they sponsor federal lobbying initiatives. If so, attend and support the initiatives focused on educating your congressional representatives about the need for stronger high schools.

- Ask your congressional representatives to increase federal funding for high schools.

- Visit The Alliance for Excellent Education to sign up for updates about national high school reform initiatives and congressional action alerts.

How Business Leaders Can Make a Difference

At the Local Level

- Convene an ongoing business roundtable examining the performance of high schools in your city or town.

- Establish partnerships with local high schools that provide internship opportunities, training resources, and other supports for schools, educators, and students.

- Sponsor an education leadership summit that brings together educators, administrators, parents, and community leaders to discuss and develop an action plan for high school reform.

- Host a meeting of local school district superintendents to find out whether the district has plans to implement high school reforms.

- Work with local officials and school district superintendents to coordinate high school curricula and activities with desired workforce skills.

At the State Level

- Convene an ongoing business roundtable examining the performance of high schools in your state.

- Host a meeting between business leaders, the state's chief school officer, and the governor to discuss how to achieve high school reform.

- Connect to or create a business/education partnership to advance school improvement.

- Work with state officials to develop a plan of action to increase graduation rates and improve the skills of the state's workforce.

- Educate state elected officials about the relationship between quality high schools and workforce preparedness and the need for high school reforms.

- Connect with an existing "P–20" Council that coordinates state education from pre-kindergarten through graduate education, or ask the governor to establish one.

At the National Level

- Educate your congressional representatives about the relationship between quality high schools and workforce preparedness and the need for twenty-first-century secondary school reforms.

- Ask your congressional representatives to increase federal funding support for high schools.

- Visit The Alliance for Excellent Education to sign up for updates about national high school reform initiatives and congressional action alerts.

Web Sites and Organizations Devoted to Children, Schools, and Education Reform

Achieve Inc.

www.achieve.org

Created in 1996 by the nation's governors and corporate leaders, Achieve is an independent, bipartisan, nonprofit education reform organization based in Washington, D.C., that helps states raise academic standards and graduation requirements, improve assessments, and strengthen accountability.

Achievement First

www.achievementfirst.org

A nonprofit charter management organization that operates a growing network of high-performing, college-preparatory, K–12 public charter schools in Connecticut and New York. The mission of Achievement First is to deliver on the promise of equal educational opportunity for all of America's children. Achievement First schools will provide all of their students with the academic and character skills they need to graduate from top colleges, to succeed in a competitive world, and to serve as the next generation of leaders for our communities.

Alliance for College-Ready Public Schools

www.laalliance.org

Alliance for College-Ready Public Schools was formed as a nonprofit charter management organization working to create a network of small, high-performing 6–8 and 9–12 public schools in some of the neediest areas of Los Angeles.

The Alliance for Educational Justice

www.allianceforeducationaljustice.org

The Alliance for Educational Justice is a national alliance of youth organizing and intergenerational groups working for educational justice. The groups in the alliance are united by the common frameworks of human and civil rights, and are working on issues that include fighting to improve college access and advocating for youth voices in school governance, presenting alternatives to punitive school discipline, and preventing the criminalization of student behavior.

The Alliance for Excellent Education

www.all4ed.org

A Washington, D.C.-based national policy and advocacy organization that works to improve national and federal policy so that all students can achieve at high academic levels and graduate high school ready for success in college, work, and citizenship in the twenty-first century.

America's Promise Alliance

www.americaspromise.org

A cross-sector partnership of more than three hundred corporations, nonprofits, faith-based organizations, and advocacy groups that are passionate about improving lives and changing outcomes for children. The work of the alliance involves raising awareness, encouraging action, and engaging in advocacy to provide children the key supports they call the Five Promises: caring adults, safe places, a healthy start, an effective education, and opportunities to help others.

Aspire Public Schools

www.aspirepublicschools.org

A nonprofit organization that has helped prepare thousands of low-income, immigrant, and minority students in elementary and secondary grades to attend college. Since its founding in 1999, Aspire has helped low-income, immigrant, and minority students beat the odds. The 6,300 students enrolled in the Aspire network are often the first in their families to even consider college, let alone get accepted to top schools such as the University of California system.

Bellwether Education

www.bellwethereducation.org

A national nonprofit organization dedicated to accelerating the achievement of low-income students by cultivating, advising, and placing a robust community of innovative, effective, and sustainable change agents in public education reform and improving the policy climate for their work.

Big Brothers Big Sisters

www.bbbs.org

As the oldest, largest, and most effective youth mentoring organization in the United States, Big Brothers Big Sisters has been the leader in one-to-one youth service for more than a century, developing positive relationships that have direct and lasting impact on the lives of young people. Big Brothers Big Sisters mentors children, ages six through eighteen, in communities across the country.

Behind the Wheel of the Bookmobile

www.bookmobiletravels.com

Behind the Wheel of the Bookmobile is a multimedia, documentary film project by Tom Corwin that follows a classic bookmobile across the country on back roads with acclaimed authors taking turns at the wheel. At each stop the bookmobile's doors will open, inviting the public to take their choice of digital and analog titles in exchange for interviews about books that have changed their lives.

Boyle Heights Learning Collaborative

www.bhlc.net

The Boyle Heights Learning Collaborative (BHLC) is a community-centered school reform effort undertaken by a wide range of community leaders. The underlying theory of the BHLC is that schools cannot improve alone and that school renewal must be accompanied by an aggressive community renewal initiative.

Boys & Girls Clubs

www.bgca.org

Boys & Girls Clubs of America had its beginnings in 1860 with several women in Hartford, Connecticut, believing that boys who roamed the streets should have a positive alternative. A cause was born with each club's efforts in enabling young people, especially those in need, to reach their full potential as productive, caring, responsible citizens.

Business Roundtable

www.businessroundtable.org

An association of chief executive officers of leading U.S. companies with nearly $6 trillion in annual revenues and more than 12 million employees. Member companies compose nearly a third of the total value of the U.S. stock markets and more than 60 percent of all corporate income taxes paid to the federal government. Annually, they return $167 billion in dividends to shareholders and the economy.

California Charter School Association

www.myschool.org

The California Charter Schools Association is California's largest charter school service organization. The association is the public voice for its members and the charter school movement in California. The association's goal is to unite the charter school community behind a common vision by providing charter schools with the resources and support to take the movement to the next level. The association has four main areas of focus: core strength, advocacy, quality, and leadership.

Center for American Progress

www.americanprogress.org

Founded in 2003 to provide long-term leadership and support to the progressive movement, the Center for American Progress (CAP) is dedicated to improving the lives of Americans through progressive ideas and action. Building on the achievements of progressive pioneers such as Teddy Roosevelt and Martin Luther King Jr., CAP's work addresses twenty-first-century challenges such as energy, national security, economic growth and opportunity, immigration, education, and health care.

Center for Education Reform

www.edreform.com

The Center for Education Reform drives the creation of better educational opportunities for all children by leading parents, policy makers and the media in boldly advocating for school choice, advancing the charter school movement, and challenging the education establishment. Through its storehouse of data and unique insights into American communities, CER uses information to turn parents into activists, policy makers into advocates, and educators into reform leaders.

Center on Education Policy

www.cep-dc.org

The Center on Education Policy is a national, independent advocate for public education and for more effective public schools. The center helps Americans better understand the role of public education in a democracy and the need to improve the academic quality of public schools.

Charter School Growth Fund

www.chartergrowthfund.org

The Charter School Growth Fund (CSGF) is a social venture investment firm that invests in high-quality charter school networks that want to grow. The Charter School Growth Fund's goal is to create 100,000 new seats for underserved children at excellent charter schools across the country. To reach its ambitious goal, CSGF funds growing charter school networks, not individual schools. In a charter network, a central office provides management support to network schools in such areas as finance, operations, and facilities, enabling the schools to focus on educating students.

Children's Defense Fund

www.childrensdefense.org

The Children's Defense Fund is a nonprofit child advocacy organization that has worked relentlessly for more than thirty-five years to ensure a level playing field for all children. CDF champions policies and programs that lift children out of poverty; protect them from abuse and neglect; and ensure their access to health care, quality education, and a moral and spiritual foundation.

Civic Builders

www.civicbuilders.org

Civic Builders is a nonprofit facilities developer that provides turnkey real estate solutions for high-performing charter schools. By assuming responsibility for building financing, acquisition, design, and construction, Civic relieves charter schools of the burden of navigating a complex real estate market and provides affordable educational facilities.

Citizen Schools

www.citizenschools.org

Citizen Schools partners with middle schools to expand the learning day for low-income children across the country. Since 1995, students at Citizen Schools have developed the academic and leadership skills they need to succeed in high school, college, the workplace, and civic life.

Communities in Schools

www.communitiesinschools.org

Communities in Schools (CIS) is the nation's largest dropout prevention organization. The mission of CIS is to champion the connection of needed community resources with schools to help young people successfully learn, stay in school, and prepare for life. By bringing caring adults into the schools to address children's unmet needs, CIS provides the link between educators and the community. The result: Teachers are free to teach, and students—many in jeopardy of dropping out—have the opportunity to focus on learning.

Community Coalition (LA)

www.cocosouthla.org

Community leaders founded Community Coalition as a non-profit organization in 1990 in response to the 1980s crack cocaine epidemic that devastated South Los Angeles. The goal is to provide preventive community-centered solutions to the drug problem.

Community Partners

www.communitypartners.org

Community Partners acts as a catalyst for community change and civic action and readiness by offering critical support, guidance, and training to a range of nonprofit organizations, initiatives, foundations, government agencies, and social entrepreneurs with innovative ideas for building communities.

DC Public Education Fund

www.dceducationfund.org

The DC Public Education Fund's mission is to dramatically improve student achievement in the District of Columbia by serving as a strategic partner to businesses, foundations, community leaders, and individual donors in supporting and investing in high-impact programs with the District of Columbia Public Schools.

Democrats for Education Reform

www.dfer.org

Democrats for Education Reform (DFER) aims to return the Democratic Party to its rightful place as a champion of children, first and foremost, in America's public education systems. DFER supports leaders in the Democratic Party who have the courage to challenge a failing status quo and who believe that the severity of our nation's educational crisis demands that this problem is tackled using every tool available.

Do Something

www.dosomething.org

Do Something believes teenagers and young people everywhere can improve their communities. Do Something leverages communications technologies to enable teens to convert their ideas and energy into action. It is their aim to inspire, empower, and celebrate a generation of doers: young people who recognize the need to do something, believe in their ability to get it done, and then take action.

Donors Choose

www.donorschoose.org

A United States–based nonprofit organization that provides a way for people to donate directly to specific projects at public schools. DC's mission is to improve public education by empowering every teacher to be a change maker and enabling any citizen to be a philanthropist.

Education Equality Project

www.educationequalityproject.org

Founded in 2008 as a national advocacy group focused on closing the achievement gap in education, Education Equality Project (EEP) is a nonpartisan group of elected officials, civil rights leaders, and education reformers working to bring equity to public education. The partnership and shared passion of these leaders—who hail from across the country and across the aisle—is the heart of the organization.

Education Trust

www.edtrust.org

The Education Trust promotes high academic achievement for all students at all levels—pre-kindergarten through college. The goal is to close the gaps in opportunity and achievement that consign far too many young people—especially those from low-income families or who are black, Latino, or American Indian—to lives on the margins of the American mainstream.

First Book

www.firstbook.org

By providing new books to children in preschools and after-school programs, mentoring and tutoring programs, shelters, day care centers and beyond, First Book provides resources to empower teachers and administrators. With access to high-quality books, educational materials, and more, these caring leaders can better teach, plan curriculum, and impart a love of learning, elevating the quality of the programs and opportunities available to children in need.

The Gates Foundation

www.gatesfoundation.org

Guided by the belief that every life has equal value, the Bill & Melinda Gates Foundation works to help all people lead healthy, productive lives. In developing countries, it focuses on improving people's health and giving them the chance to lift themselves out of hunger and extreme poverty. In the United States, it seeks to ensure that all people—especially those with the fewest resources—have access to the opportunities they need to succeed in school and life. Based in Seattle, Washington, the foundation is led by CEO Jeff Raikes and Co-Chair William H. Gates Sr., under the direction of Bill and Melinda Gates and Warren Buffett.

Get Schooled

www.getschooled.com

Get Schooled is a national program that connects, inspires, and mobilizes people to work harder to increase high school and college graduation rates, improve postsecondary readiness, and promote the fundamental importance of education. With specific elements targeted at everyone from policy makers and corporate leaders to communities and kids, it's an interlocking system of actions, including community initiatives, programming, corporate and philanthropic partnerships, and an online portal. It provides resources and information, community outreach, and creative programming that engages the audiences who are affected by America's ongoing educational crisis. Developed in partnership with the Bill & Melinda Gates Foundation, the initiative pairs the foundation's deep knowledge of education reform with the incredible reach and unmatched creativity of its brands and partners to bring a new level of awareness and engagement to this critical issue.

Girl Scouts of the USA

www.girlscouts.org

Founded in 1912, Girl Scouts of the USA is dedicated to building girls of courage, confidence, and character who make the world a better place. The preeminent leadership development organization for girls, it has 3.4 million child and adult members worldwide. Its leadership program offers many correlations to school curriculum standards for all fifty states. Girl Scouts of the USA has received international recognition for research and public policy information related to the development and well-being of girls through its Girl Scout Research Institute, which was launched in 2000.

Grad Nation

www.americaspromise.org/Our-Work/Dropout-Prevention/ Grad-Nation-Campaign.aspx

On March 1, 2010, General Colin Powell, America's Promise Alliance Chair Alma Powell, and U.S. Secretary of Education Arne Duncan were joined by President Barack Obama to announce the formation of Grad Nation. Grad Nation is a ten-year campaign to mobilize the nation as never before to reverse the dropout crisis and enable children to be prepared for success in college, work, and life. The goals of this campaign are to ensure that 90 percent of today's fourth graders graduate high school on time and to help fulfill the president's pledge to be the world's leader in the proportion of college graduates by 2020.

GreatSchools

www.greatschools.org

GreatSchools is the country's leading source of information on school performance. With listings of 200,000 public and private schools serving students from preschool through high school and more than 800,000 parent ratings and reviews, GreatSchools has become the go-to guide for parents aiming to make a smart school choice.

Green Dot Schools

www.greendot.org

Steve Barr founded Green Dot Public Schools in 1999 in direct response to the terrible state of public high schools in the Los Angeles area. Barr started Green Dot with a vision of leveraging charter schools as a tool to show the school district and the public at large that there was a more effective way to provide public education to young adults in the Los Angeles area. Green Dot Public Schools is now leading the charge to transform public education in Los Angeles and beyond so that all children receive the education they need to be successful in college, leadership, and life.

Harlem Children's Zone

www.hcz.org

Harlem Children's Zone is a community-based organization serving more than 17,000 children living in a 100-city-block area in

Harlem, New York City. HCZ has pioneered a new way to end the cycle of generational poverty with programs that support each child from before birth all the way through college—bringing educated young adults back into their communities to enrich it.

Harlem Success Academy

www.harlemsuccess.org

Success Charter Network is an ambitious management network of four high-performing charter schools in New York City, including Harlem Success Academy. The best teachers from around the country teach Harlem Success Scholars, their progress is assessed every eight weeks, and all children who need it are given targeted one-on-one tutoring by highly trained tutors to ensure they progress at the highest of levels.

Hope Street Group

www.hopestreetgroup.org

As a new generation of leaders dedicated to building an opportunity economy, Hope Street Group builds diverse coalitions from their own network of business, civil society, and political leaders to drive innovative policies that make economic opportunity possible for all Americans.

KIPP Schools

www.kipp.org

Knowledge Is Power Program (KIPP) is a national network of free, open-enrollment, college-preparatory public schools with a track record of preparing students in underserved communities for success in college and in life. Eighty-two KIPP schools in nineteen states and the District of Columbia serve more than 21,000 students.

Leadership Conference on Civil and Human Rights & Leadership Conference Education Fund

www.civilrights.org

A coalition charged by its diverse membership of more than two hundred national organizations to promote and protect the civil and human rights of all persons in the United States. Through advocacy and outreach to targeted constituencies, the Leadership Conference works toward the goal of a more open and just society—an America as good as its ideals.

The Learning Alliance

www.learningfirst.org

A permanent partnership of eighteen leading education associations with more than 10 million members dedicated to improving student learning in America's public schools, the Learning Alliance shares examples of success, encourages collaboration at every level, and works toward the continual and long-term improvement of public education based on solid research.

MENTOR

www.mentoring.org

For more than a decade, MENTOR/National Mentoring Partnership has been working to expand the world of quality mentoring. MENTOR believes that, with the help and guidance of an adult mentor, each child can discover how to unlock and achieve his or her potential. MENTOR is widely acknowledged as the nation's premier advocate and resource for expanding mentoring initiatives nationwide. As such, MENTOR works with a strong network of state and local mentoring partnerships to leverage resources and provide the support and tools that mentoring organizations need to effectively serve young people in their communities.

Milk + Bookies

www.milkandbookies.com

Milk + Bookies is a nationwide charitable organization that inspires children to give back, using books as its currency. At Milk + Bookies events, boys and girls are provided the opportunity to select, purchase, and inscribe books that are then donated to their peers who do not have access to books of their own. The fun-filled events feature music, story time, and, of course, milk and cookies. Milk + Bookies combines two essential and worthwhile efforts: literacy promotion and service learning. While the book donations are imperative to their mission, just as important is instilling the seed of giving into each host and the young guests, sparking feelings of importance, self-confidence, and the desire to give and give again.

National Alliance for Charter Schools

www.publiccharters.org

As the leading national nonprofit organization committed to advancing the charter school movement, the alliance's goal is to increase the number of high-quality charter schools available to all families, particularly in disadvantaged communities that lack access to quality public schools. The alliance provides assistance to state charter school associations and resource centers, develops and advocates for improved public policies, and serves as the united voice for this large and diverse movement.

New Leaders for New Schools

www.nlns.org

Founded in 2000 by a team of social entrepreneurs, New Leaders attracts, prepares, and supports outstanding individuals to become the next generation of school leaders in response to the immense need for exceptional principals in our nation's urban public schools. More than a principal training program, New Leaders for New Schools is a national movement of leaders with an unwavering commitment to ensure that every student achieves academic excellence.

NewSchools Venture Fund

www.newschools.org

NewSchools Venture Fund seeks to transform public education through powerful ideas and passionate entrepreneurs so that all children—especially those in underserved communities—have the opportunity to succeed. A national nonprofit venture philanthropy firm founded in 1998, NewSchools has invested in more than thirty-five nonprofit and for-profit organizations and raised more than $175 million. In addition to helping these entrepreneurs create and grow sustainable organizations that deliver great results for students and communities, NewSchools also connects educational entrepreneurs with one another to accelerate the broader pace of change throughout public education.

New York Charter School Association

www.nycsa.org

Serving more than eighty charter schools, the association is the leading advocate, supporter, connector, and catalyst for high-performing schools across New York state. The New York Charter School Association's model and services empower member schools to operate more efficiently, educators to teach more effectively, students to improve academic performance, funding partners to give with more impact, and elected officials to shape policies that support these goals.

New Visions for Public Schools

www.newvisions.org

Throughout its twenty-year history, New Visions has worked intensively with a core group of schools while fashioning strategies to improve student achievement across the board. Today, with seventy-six schools serving more than 34,000 students, New Visions supports a network similar in size to some of the nation's largest school districts. The organization is committed to proving that large numbers of urban students can graduate on time and be successful in college and in the workplace.

Parent Revolution

www.parentrevolution.org

Parent Revolution was started by a coalition of organizations, led by the Los Angeles Parents Union (LAPU). LAPU was founded in 2006 as a coalition of parents who had tired of sending their kids to broken schools. In LAPU's view, it is time for parents, as the only ones who will always stand up for their children, no matter what, to take back their power over education.

Partnership to Uplift Communities

www.pucschools.org

The mission at Partnership to Uplift Communities (PUC) schools is to develop and manage high-quality charter schools in densely populated urban communities with overcrowded and low-achieving schools. PUC schools create programs and cultures that result in college graduation for all students. By focusing on developing secondary schools partnered with strong feeder elementary programs, PUC uplifts and revitalizes communities through the development of educational and other supportive partnerships.

The Philadelphia Student Union

www.phillystudentunion.org

The Philadelphia Student Union exists to build the power of young people to demand a high-quality education in the Philadelphia public school system. A youth-led organization, it seeks to make positive changes in the short term by helping youth learn how to organize to build power. The youth become lifelong learners and leaders who can bring diverse groups of people together to address the problems that their schools and communities face.

Project GRAD

www.projectgrad.org

Project GRAD believes that every student, regardless of ethnicity or socioeconomic background, not only deserves to, but should graduate from high school and have access to college. Because of this fundamental belief in the equality of expectations for every at-risk child, Project GRAD sets what might be considered by some to be lofty goals. Yet, Project GRAD's goals are the standard for the average student who attends a school in a higher socioeconomic neighborhood.

Public Education Network

www.publiceducation.org

Public Education Network (PEN) is a national association of local education funds and *individuals* working to advance public school reform in low-income communities across the country. PEN believes an active, vocal constituency is the key to ensuring that every child, in every community, benefits from a quality public education.

Reach Out and Read

www.reachoutandread.org

Reach Out and Read is an evidence-based nonprofit organization that promotes early literacy and school readiness in pediatric exam rooms nationwide by giving new books to children and advice to parents about the importance of reading aloud. Doctors, nurse practitioners, and other medical professionals incorporate Reach Out and Read's evidence-based model into regular pediatric checkups by advising parents about the importance of reading aloud and giving developmentally-appropriate books to children, beginning at the six-month checkup and continuing through age five.

Room to Read

www.roomtoread.org

Room to Read seeks to transform the lives of millions of children in the developing world by focusing on literacy and gender equality in education. Working in collaboration with local communities, partner organizations, and governments, we develop literacy skills and a habit of reading among primary school children and ensure girls have the skills and support needed to complete their secondary education.

The San Francisco Education Fund

www.sffund.org

The San Francisco Education Fund's programming focuses on one goal: improving student success in San Francisco public schools. Competitive grants are made to teams of teachers that focus on a specific issue, such as improving literacy, at their school. Teacher teams are trained to use student data to inform their work and are provided with on-site coaching throughout the yearlong grant. The fund also offers teacher residencies, where aspiring teachers integrate their master's level course work with an intensive, full-year classroom residency alongside an experienced mentor.

Scholastic

www.scholastic.com

For nearly ninety years, Scholastic has recognized the importance of working with public, private, and nonprofit organizations that share its mission and goals to improve the well-being of children. Scholastic's total commitment to social responsibility and educational outreach is demonstrated by its diverse partnerships, which address today's most critical issues facing communities, with an emphasis on reading and literacy.

SEED

www.seedfoundation.com

The SEED Foundation is a national nonprofit that partners with urban communities to provide innovative educational opportunities that prepare underserved students for success in college and beyond. The SEED Foundation is a catalyst for change in urban education: It developed the SEED boarding school model and opened its first school, the SEED School of Washington, D.C., in 1998. Its second school opened in Maryland in August 2008.

The Sesame Workshop

www.sesameworkshop.org

Formerly known as the Children's Television Workshop, the Sesame Workshop is a worldwide American nonprofit organization behind the production of several educational children's programs that have run on public broadcasting around the world (including PBS in the United States).

The Skoll Foundation

www.skollfoundation.org

The Skoll Foundation drives large-scale change by investing in, connecting, and celebrating social entrepreneurs and other innovators dedicated to solving the world's most pressing problems.

The foundation's vision is to live in a sustainable world of peace and prosperity: "Uncommon heroes, common good."

Stand for Children

www.stand.org

An innovative, grassroots child advocacy organization, Stand for Children's mission is to use the power of grassroots action to help all children get the excellent public education and strong support they need to thrive. Following specific priorities chosen by its members, the organization focuses on securing adequate funding for public schools and reforming education policies and practices to help children thrive academically, giving them the opportunities they need to become successful, productive citizens.

Teach For America

www.teachforamerica.org

The national corps of outstanding recent college graduates of all academic majors and career interests who commit two years to teach in urban and rural public schools and become leaders in the effort to expand educational opportunity.

The New Teacher Project

www.tntp.org

Founded by teachers, The New Teacher Project was formed in 1997 to address the growing issues of teacher shortages and teacher quality throughout the country. In its first year, TNTP embarked on three projects to create and implement high-quality alternative routes to certification programs to bring new streams of accomplished individuals into hard-to-staff urban schools. Since then, TNTP has worked with more than two hundred school districts and become a nationally recognized authority on new teacher recruitment and hiring.

Thomas B. Fordham Institute

www.edexcellence.net

A Washington, D.C.-based nonprofit think tank dedicated to advancing educational excellence in America's K–12 schools, the Fordham Institute promotes policies that strengthen accountability and expand education options for parents and families and examines issues such as the No Child Left Behind Act, school choice, and teacher quality.

United Way Worldwide

www.unitedway.org/worldwide

Unlike other nongovernmental organizations, United Ways around the world engage all sectors—public, private, and civil society—at the community level, mobilizing individuals so they become change agents in their own communities to improve the conditions in which they live. By working at the local level, the United Way movement addresses the root cause of issues that affect families and individuals.

United Negro College Fund

www.uncf.org

An educational assistance organization with forty private, historically black member colleges and universities. The UNCF administers four hundred scholarship and internship programs, so that even students from low- and moderate-income families can afford college tuition, books, and room/board. The UNCF also serves as a national advocate for the importance of minority higher education by representing the public policy interests of its students and member colleges.

Walden Media

www.walden.com

Walden Media specializes in entertainment for the whole family. Past award-winning films include the *Chronicles of Narnia* series, *Journey to the Center of the Earth*, *Nim's Island*, and *Charlotte's Web*. Upcoming films include *Ramona & Beezus*, based on the best-selling book series by Beverly Cleary and starring Selena Gomez, and the latest installment in the *Narnia* series, *The Chronicles of Narnia: The Voyage of the Dawn Treader*.

Mom Congress Lesson Plan
for Change: Will You Be a Hero
for Education?

The Editors of Parenting *Magazine*[*]

Found: 51 amazing moms.

In 2009, we at *Parenting* formed Mom Congress on Education and Learning, a grassroots coalition that connects and celebrates moms making a difference in their children's schools, so they can share the lessons they've learned and encourage other moms to advocate for positive educational change. Next, we launched our "Send a Mom to Congress" contest at the beginning of 2010 and chose a representative from each state and the District of Columbia. We flew them to Georgetown University in Washington, D.C., this past May, where they spent two days meeting with and listening to a stellar lineup of panelists, including U.S. Secretary of Education Arne Duncan, National PTA CEO Byron Garrett, National Education Association vice president Lily Eskelsen, and faculty from Georgetown

*Reprinted with permission from the October 2010 issue of *Parenting School Years* magazine.

University's School of Continuing Studies, the Mom Congress educational provider.

The task at hand: develop a "Lesson Plan for Change" to empower moms everywhere to fight to improve their children's schools. Whether it's a little issue (say, you want to outfit every classroom with a new book series) or a big one (maybe you want to secure funding for additional special education teachers or build a new gymnasium or computer lab), you can follow this road map. It was drawn up by these seasoned movers and shakers who've used the very same strategies to mobilize their own communities and convince school boards and administrators that it's time for a change. Look at what they've accomplished:

- Gwen Eaddy-Samuel of Meriden, Connecticut, founded the first child pedestrian safety program in her town for kids walking to public and private school.

- Myrdin Thompson of Louisville, Kentucky, led a successful effort to build a new playground and garden at her children's school that netted a $15,000 grant from KaBOOM, a national nonprofit (more on it later!). Then she raised an additional $50,000 from the community.

- Delegate Jennifer DeFranco of Palatine, Illinois, secured a proclamation signed by the state governor deeming one week in October to be Bullying Prevention Awareness Week; schools around the state participated with related programs.

- Virginia delegate Christine Morin of Lorton fought and won not just one but two battles for the construction of new schools in Fairfax County.

"We are going to win the fight for better schools when passionate moms put the power of their citizenship to work," the NEA's Lily Eskelsen told these amazing Mom Congress delegates. Are you ready to join their ranks? Let's get started!

Step 1: Build Your Case

So you have a problem with your child's school. It's easy to wait around for someone else to notice and take action. But you're a passionate mom, too, and don't want that to happen after your child has moved on. You need to get the ball rolling now—change always takes time.

First, identify your goal. Let's say your school's playground has outdated equipment that may be inadequate for the number of students or even dangerous. Worse yet, maybe your school doesn't even have a playground. You want to find funding to build a state-of-the-art outdoor play space that will not only be fun for the kids, but also get them moving. And that, in turn, will keep them healthy and therefore *will help them learn.*

Form a strategy team. Start talking about your concern with your immediate circle of parents and get them on board with your ideas. Think about who your "heavy lifters" could be—the parents who would be willing to not just sign a petition but really spend time on your cause. Is there someone who's good at and enjoys social media? How about an artistic mom who might design posters and flyers? Someone who knows how to write grant letters that could help secure funding for your new playground? Perhaps most important, who will be your spokesperson? Maybe it's you, but maybe it's someone else who has experience as a persuasive speaker and enjoys taking center stage.

Do your research. To convince your school board that your cause is a critical one, you'll need studies and statistics and personal stories from parents and kids to back up your idea. Reach out to specific advocacy groups that have information on the importance of recess and how it impacts learning. KaBOOM, a national nonprofit dedicated to creating play spaces in communities that lack them, is one such group. Safe Kids USA is another that has lots of background information on safe play structures and practices. Perhaps a local pediatric practice or children's hospital concerned about childhood obesity would be willing to back your campaign. And don't forget about your local community leaders: Maybe that playground could be used as part of a summer camp program that would benefit others in the town.

Next, do some number crunching: How much would your new playground cost? Get a copy of your school budget and analyze it for possible funds. Who might be willing to contribute to your cause: That children's hospital? Your town council? How about a local builder? What would construction costs typically run, and is there a contractor who may be willing to donate his time or at least do the work for less than the going rate?

Finally, consider the opposing viewpoint: Why wouldn't your board want to build a new playground? How will you convince them otherwise? If it's a matter of money (and almost everything is), will you be able to secure enough without dipping into the school budget?

Work together with your group to create a mission statement. This brief but formal description of your goal will provide a sense of direction for your cause and guide decision making. For example:

Our mission is to build a fun and safe state-of-the-art playground for the students of Lincoln Elementary School and the surrounding community. Our goal is to raise the necessary funds and secure approval to begin construction by the summer of 2011, so that the playground will be completed by the opening of school in September.

Develop an "elevator pitch." If you had to explain your cause and convince someone of its importance while riding in an elevator, what exactly would you say? Could you make a convincing case in only a minute or two? For example:

Do you realize that students at Lincoln Elementary don't get outdoor recess because the playground is unsafe? It was built in 1972, and the principal is concerned that somebody could get hurt on the dilapidated equipment. Unfortunately, research shows that no recess means not only no exercise for these kids, but that their grades are likely to drop a full ten points. We've formed a committee that's working toward securing funding for a new playground. Would you sign our petition or attend our meeting this Tuesday evening?

Lobby your principal, teachers, and district superintendent. The support of your school leaders will be an important component when you present your case to the school board. In addition, they may know of other people or groups in your school community who are interested in the same cause and with whom you can join forces.

Step 2: Create Your Coalition and Spread the Word

Now that you have your foundation and key players in place, it's time to inform—and motivate—the school community to join your cause. There are two main keys to success: Spread the word in as many ways as you can and give parents lots of options for getting involved.

Create a fact sheet that outlines the main points in your case. Use your elevator pitch as your guide. You can add in more specifics (such as the research that shows how regular recess/exercise improves kids' grades) as well as how much it will cost. Most important: Keep it to one page. You'll lose 'em after that!

Brand your message. Your job is to sell people on your cause, and when you have a snappy, memorable slogan, you stand a greater chance of getting the message to stick. Tap the artistic members on your strategy team and ask them to design a logo or icon that you'll be able to use on your Facebook page (see below) and on signs, flyers, etc.

Start a Facebook page. Or a Web site. Or a Twitter account. Or all three! You'll want a central place where people can go to get all the detailed info about your project. Here's where you'll post not only your fact sheet, but also all your supporting documents, details about events and fund raisers, updates on your progress . . . you get the picture. You can invite people to download your logo to display on their own pages. As your fans grow, you'll be able to quickly inform the masses. Social media outreach also gives the parents who care—but may not have the time or ability to help in a big way—an opportunity to stay involved and up to date. They may not be able to attend a rally or a meeting, but they can sign an online petition (next!) and share their personal experiences with the group at large.

Launch a petition drive. There's nothing like a long list of names to prove that people care about an issue. You'll want to collect them from all fronts, so along with posting a petition on-line, plan to hit the bricks, too. Set up a table (with permission) outside the local grocery store or coffee shop. Walk the pick-up line after school. Knock on some doors. You can't have too much support.

Have coffee with the board. It's smart to reach out to the individual members of your school board, especially the ones who might be particularly passionate about or sympathetic to your project. You'll want to focus on the bottom line: how the kids, the community—and the budget—will benefit long-term.

Loop in your PTA/PTO. Ask to give a brief presentation during one of the meetings. You'll have a captive, engaged audience who will likely be eager to help you get the word out.

Build local alliances. See a pattern? Building your coalition is all about the schmoozing. If you've got a project that will benefit the town at large (such as a playground, pool, or other new facility), set up meetings with local business owners as well as local government officials. You never know how they may be able to lend support, whether it's with direct funding, construction supplies, free printing or design work, or event support.

Contact local media. Designate a member of the team to handle public relations, and ask her to draw up a press release you can send to the local education reporters for your TV stations and newspaper. (Another place your fact sheet will come in handy.) For greatest impact, keep your press release under a page in length. Just as important: Be sure your outreach includes your local parent bloggers—even if they're not in your district, chances are they have fans who are.

Brainstorm fund raisers and research possible grants. You know you probably won't get the district to pony up all the cash you need, especially for an expensive project like a playground. So now's the time to figure out where and how you can start raising the cash. These details will be necessary when you present your case to the board.

Step 3: Take Your Plan to the School Board

The school board is the group that holds the purse strings—and the power to green-light new projects. You'll need to prepare a strong presentation to snag their votes. What you'll need to do:

Recruit audience support. Get the word out to other parents in your community that it's showtime—you want as many people as possible standing behind you at the presentation (figuratively speaking). Think of ways parents who may not be available for that event can help out: Maybe they can give out something symbolic, such as a pencil, an apple, or a mini water bottle, along with a flyer about your cause during drop-off or pick-up the next day to continue the momentum.

Write your script. This was a universal piece of advice among the Mom Congress delegates. It will help you stay on point—and stay concise. These tips can help you structure your speech:

- Start with a general overview (base it on your elevator pitch).

- Back it up with your supporting data on how the project will save money and/or improve learning long-term.

- Offer a real-life anecdote or two to make the issue personal.

  - Wrap it up with a memorable sound bite—namely, your slogan!

(For more great advice, check out the tool kits on KeepArtsin Schools.org, which can be applied to any cause.)

Be prepared to debate and defend your position. (See the importance of research above!) Anticipate the questions and know how you'll answer them. Depending on how much opposition you expect, you may even want to hold a mock meeting with your strategy team to practice making your points.

Maintain a friendly and courteous tone. Seems obvious, but you actually *will* catch more flies with honey.

Say "thank you" twice! Of course you'll thank the board for their time at the end, but it's also smart to follow up with a letter. Not only does it push the sugar factor, but it also keeps your issue top of mind.

Leave materials behind. Give each board member a copy of your talking points and any relevant backup to have on hand during deliberations.

Rally your troops. If you can, plan to gather at least your strategy team for a postmortem and to keep motivation running high. Because no matter what happens this round, you know you'll keep fighting for what your kids need—and deserve!

• • •

Join the fight for better schools today! To become a member of *Parenting*'s Mom Congress coalition, visit Parenting.com/momcongress for more information.

• • •

Contributors:

Linda Payne, *Alabama*
Leesa Arnes, *Alaska*
Christina Hernandez, *Arizona*
Melanie Fox, *Arkansas*
Laura Taylor, *California*
Virginia Zimmerman, *Colorado*
Gwen Samuels, *Connecticut*
Debra Heffernan, *Delaware*
Jennifer Shirah, *Florida*
Michelle Kelly, *Georgia*
Becky Staley, *Hawaii*
Jamie Pearce, *Idaho*
Jennifer DeFranco, *Illinois*
Bonnie DeLong, *Indiana*
Shellie Pike, *Iowa*
Carrie Petruncola, *Kansas*
Myrdin Thompson, *Kentucky*
Erin Jones, *Louisiana*
Catherine Anderson, *Maine*
Bernardette Jones, *Maryland*
Heather Jack, *Massachusetts*
Luanne Goffnett, *Michigan*
Chanda Kropp, *Minnesota*
Deloris Irving, *Mississippi*
Kim Acuff, *Missouri*
Susie Hamilton, *Montana*
Brea Kniss, *Nebraska*

Dena Bodecker, *Nevada*
Angeline Gorham, *New Hampshire*
Karyn White, *New Jersey*
Elizabeth Prishkulnik, *New Mexico*
Amie Hamlin, *New York*
Liza Weidle, *North Carolina*
Cheryl Lausch, *North Dakota*
Emily Rempe, *Ohio*
Sheila Groves, *Oklahoma*
Tonjia Haskins, *Oregon*
Melissa Bilash, *Pennsylvania*
Jennifer Quigley-Harris, *Rhode Island*
Yolanda Gordon, *South Carolina*
Bobbie Wirth, *South Dakota*
O. Pearl Andrews, *Tennessee*
Sybille White, *Texas*
Lori Harding, *Utah*
Dawn Moskowitz, *Vermont*
Christine Morin, *Virginia*
Trisha Novotny, *Washington*
Nadine Duplessy Kearns, *Washington, DC*
Carrie Clendening, *West Virginia*
Stacey Kannenburg, *Wisconsin*
Jennifer Allison, *Wyoming*

NOTES

Chapter 3

1. *Multiple Choice: Charter School Performance in 16 States*, http://credo
.stanford.edu/reports/MULTIPLE_CHOICE_CREDO.pdf.

Chapter 5

1. Reviews of the statistical analyses behind these findings can be found in
Eric A. Hanushek and Steven G. Rivkin, "Teacher Quality," in *Handbook of the
Economics of Education*, ed. Eric A. Hanushek and Finis Welch (Amsterdam:
North Holland, 2006), pp. 1051–1078; and Eric A. Hanushek and Steven G.
Rivkin, "Generalizations about Using Value-Added Measures of Teacher Qual-
ity," *American Economic Review* 100, no. 2 (May 2010): 267–271.

2. Hanushek and Rivkin, "Generalizations about Using Value-Added
Measures."

3. The impact of higher achievement on individual income and on the national economy is reviewed in Eric A. Hanushek and Ludger Woessmann, "The
Role of Cognitive Skills in Economic Development," *Journal of Economic Litera-
ture* 46, no. 3 (September 2008): 607–668.

4. U.S. Department of Education, *Digest of Education Statistics, 2009* (Washington, DC: National Center for Education Statistics, 2010).

5. Eric A. Hanushek, "Teacher Deselection," in *Creating a New Teaching Profession*, ed. Dan Goldhaber and Jane Hannaway (Washington, DC: Urban Institute Press, 2009), pp. 165–180.

6. Michael Barber and Mona Mourshed, *How the World's Best-Performing
School Systems Come Out on Top* (McKinsey and Company, 2007).

Chapter 6

1. Lara Fabiano, Lee M. Pearson, and Imeh J. Williams, *Putting Students on a Pathway to Academic and Social Success: Phase III Findings of the Citizen Schools Evaluation*, Policy Studies Associates, November 2005, www.policystudies.com/studies/youth/CS%20Phase%20III%202005.pdf; Juliet Diehl Vile, Erikson Arcaira, and Elizabeth R. Reisner, *Progress Toward High School Graduation: Citizen Schools' Youth Outcomes in Boston*, Policy Studies Associates, July 2009, www.citizenschools.org/uploads/PSA%20Phase%20VI%20Progress%20toward%20HS%20Graduation%2020090819.pdf.

2. Nancy Morrow-Howell, et al., *Evaluation of Experience Corps: Student Reading Outcomes*, Center for Social Development, George Warren Brown School of Social Work, Washington University in St. Louis, January 2009, http://csd.wustl.edu/Publications/Documents/RP09–01.pdf.

3. Frederick Hess, *Education Unbound: The Promise and Practice of Greenfield Schooling* (Alexandria, VA: Association for Supervision & Curriculum Development, 2010).

4. Jennifer Medina, "Laptop? Check. Student Playlist? Check. Classroom of the Future? Check," *New York Times*, July 21, 2009, www.nytimes.com/2009/07/22/education/22school.html?_r=1&scp=5&sq=classroom%20of%20the%20future&st=cse; Arthur E. Levine, "The School of One: The School of Tomorrow," *Huffington Post*, September 16, 2009, www.huffingtonpost.com/arthur-e-levine/the-school-of-one-the-sch_b_288695.html.

5. "Facts and Data," Met School, www.themetschool.org/Metcenter/Facts_and_Data.html.

6. Robert Putnam, *Bowling Alone: The Collapse and Revival of American Community* (New York: Simon & Schuster, 2001), pp. 299–300.

7. "Testimonials," National Lab Day: A National Barn-Raising for Hands-On Learning, www.nationallabday.org/testimonials.

8. "Survey: Majority of U.S. Teens Feel Prepared for Careers in Science, Technology, Engineering and Mathematics, Yet Many Lack Mentors," press release, Lemelson-MIT Program, January 7, 2009, http://mit.edu/invent/n-press-releases/n-press-09index.html.

9. *The Economic Impact of the Achievement Gap in America's Schools*, Social Sector Office, McKinsey & Company, April 2009, www.mckinsey.com/App_Media/Images/Page_Images/Offices/SocialSector/PDF/achievement_gap_report.pdf.

10. Putnam, *Bowling Alone*, pp. 55–57.

Chapter 7

1. National Assessment of Educational Progress, 2007

2. DC Education Compact, DC College Access Program, DC State Education Department, and DC Public Schools, *Double the Numbers for College Success: A Call to Action for the District of Columbia*, October 2006, http://news room.dc.gov/file.aspx/release/9956/DoublingNumber_FINAL.pdf.

3. DC Comprehensive Assessment System (DC CAS) and DC Public Schools data.

4. *Dynamic Indicators of Basic Early Literacy Skills*, analysis from Wireless Generation.

5. DC CAS data, 2007–2009.

6. National Assessment of Educational Progress/Trial Urban Districts Assessment data (NAEP/TUDA), 2009.

7. NAEP/TUDA, 2009.

Chapter 8

1. Tamara Wilder, Whitney Allgood, and Richard Rothstein, *Narrowing the Achievement Gap for Low-Income Children: A 19-Year Life Cycle Approach*, prepared for the 2008 Equity Symposium of the Campaign for Education Equity, Teachers College, Columbia University, November 17–18, 2008, http://epi.3cdn.net/07bc530ac6dfe6ec1d_jkm6bhwro.pdf.

2. *Multiple Choice: Charter School Performance in 16 States* (Stanford, CA: CREDO, Stanford University, 2009), http://credo.stanford.edu/reports/MULTIPLE_CHOICE_CREDO.pdf.

3. Daniel Schorn, "The Harlem Children's Zone: How One Man's Vision to Revitalize Harlem Starts with Children," *60 Minutes*, May 14, 2006, www.cbsnews.com/stories/2006/05/11/60minutes/main1611936.shtml.

4. "Hunger and Homeless at Record Levels in U.S. Cities," U.S. Conference of Mayors, December 24, 2009, www.citymayors.com/features/uscity_poverty.html.

5. *2010 Child and Youth Well-Being Index (CWI)* (Durham, NC: Foundation for Child Development, 2010), www.fcd-us.org/usr_doc/FINAL_2010_CWI_Annual_Release.pdf.

Chapter 11

1. David Angus and Jeffrey Mirel, *The Failed Promise of the American High School 1890–1995* (New York: Teachers College Press, 1999).

2. John M. Bridgeland, John J. DiIulio Jr., and Karen Burke Morison, *The Silent Epidemic* (Washington, DC: Civic Enterprises, 2006).

3. Editorial Projects in Education, "Diplomas Count," *Education Week* 29, no. 34 (June 10, 2010).

4. Thomas Bailey, "Challenge and Opportunity: Rethinking the Role and Function of Developmental Education in Community College," CCRC Working Paper No. 14, Community College Research Center, 2008.

5. Calculations based on U.S. Census Bureau, "Educational Attainment in the United States: 2009," Current Population Survey, 2009 Annual Social and Economic Supplement, www.census.gov/population/www/socdemo/education/cps2009.html.

6. Anthony P. Carnevale, Nicole Smith, and Jeff Strohl, *Help Wanted: Projections of Jobs and Education Requirements Through 2018* (Washington, DC: Georgetown University Center on Education and the Workforce, 2010).

7. Organisation for Economic Co-operation and Development, "Indicator A2: How Many Students Finish Secondary Education and Access Tertiary Education?" in *Education at a Glance 2009: OECD Indicators* (Paris: OECD, 2009). The United States' 2007 graduation rate was eighteenth out of twenty-five OECD nations.

8. Thomas Snyder and Sally Dillow, *Digest of Education Statistics: 2009* (Washington, DC: National Center for Education Statistics, U.S. Department of Education, 2009).

9. Laura G. Knapp, Janice E. Kelly-Reid, and Scott A. Ginder, *Enrollment in Postsecondary Institutions, Fall 2008; Graduation Rates, 2002 & 2005 Cohorts; and Financial Statistics, Fiscal Year 2008* (Washington, DC: National Center for Education Statistics, U.S. Department of Education, April 2010). Note: Graduation rates are for first-time, full-time students graduating in 150 percent normal time.

10. Becky Smerdon, Barbara Means, et al., *Evaluation of the Bill & Melinda Gates Foundation's High School Grants Initiative: 2001–2005 Final Report* (Washington, DC: American Institutes for Research; Menlo Park, CA: SRI International, 2006).

11. Steven G. Rivkin, Eric A. Hanushek, and John F. Kain, "Teachers, Schools, and Academic Achievement," *Econometrica* 73, no. 2 (March 2005): 417–458.

12. Robert Gordon, Thomas J. Kane, and Douglas O. Staiger, *Identifying Effective Teachers Using Performance on the Job* (Washington, DC: Hamilton Project, Brookings Institution, 2006).

13. Stephen Newton, "Stull Evaluations and Student Performance," Los Angeles Unified School District, http://notebook.lausd.net/pls/ptl/docs/PAGE/CA_LAUSD/FLDR_ORGANIZATIONS/FLDR_PLCY_RES_DEV/PAR_DIVISION_MAIN/RESEARCH_UNIT/PUBLICATIONS/POLICY_REPORTS/IMPACT_STULL_186.PDF.

14. Kim Marshall, "It's Time to Rethink Teacher Supervision and Evaluation," *Phi Delta Kappan*, June 2005.

15. Scholastic and Bill & Melinda Gates Foundation, *Primary Sources: America's Teachers on America's Schools* (New York: Scholastic Inc., 2010).

16. Marguerite Roza, *Frozen Assets: Rethinking Teacher Contracts Could Free Billions for School Reform* (Washington, DC: Education Sector, 2007).

17. Valerie Russ, "Teachers, School District Approve Contract," *Philadelphia Daily News*, January 23, 2010.

18. Scholastic and Bill & Melinda Gates Foundation, *Primary Sources*.

19. "Rocketship Education 2009 Academic Results Highest Performing in San Jose and Santa Clara County, Tops Palo Alto Unified," www.rsed.org/news/RSED%2009%20Results%20Release%209.16%20FINAL.doc.

20. Mike Feinberg, personal communications, 2010.

INDEX

I believe that a good story well told can truly make a difference in how one sees the world. This is why I started Participant Media: to tell compelling, entertaining stories that create awareness of the real issues that shape our lives.

At Participant, we seek to entertain our audiences first, and then invite them to participate in making a difference. With each film, we create social action and advocacy programs that highlight the issues that resonate in the film and provide ways to transform the impact of the media experience into individual and community action.

Twenty-seven films later, from GOOD NIGHT, AND GOOD LUCK to AN INCONVENIENT TRUTH, and from FOOD, INC. to COUNTDOWN TO ZERO, and through thousands of social action activities, Participant continues to create entertainment that inspires and compels social change. Now through our partnership with PublicAffairs, we are extending our mission so that more of you can join us in making our world a better place.

Jeff Skoll, Founder and Chairman
Participant Media

PublicAffairs is a publishing house founded in 1997. It is a tribute to the standards, values, and flair of three persons who have served as mentors to countless reporters, writers, editors, and book people of all kinds, including me.

I. F. STONE, proprietor of *I. F. Stone's Weekly*, combined a commitment to the First Amendment with entrepreneurial zeal and reporting skill and became one of the great independent journalists in American history. At the age of eighty, Izzy published *The Trial of Socrates*, which was a national bestseller. He wrote the book after he taught himself ancient Greek.

BENJAMIN C. BRADLEE was for nearly thirty years the charismatic editorial leader of *The Washington Post*. It was Ben who gave the *Post* the range and courage to pursue such historic issues as Watergate. He supported his reporters with a tenacity that made them fearless and it is no accident that so many became authors of influential, best-selling books.

ROBERT L. BERNSTEIN, the chief executive of Random House for more than a quarter century, guided one of the nation's premier publishing houses. Bob was personally responsible for many books of political dissent and argument that challenged tyranny around the globe. He is also the founder and longtime chair of Human Rights Watch, one of the most respected human rights organizations in the world.

· · ·

For fifty years, the banner of Public Affairs Press was carried by its owner Morris B. Schnapper, who published Gandhi, Nasser, Toynbee, Truman, and about 1,500 other authors. In 1983, Schnapper was described by *The Washington Post* as "a redoubtable gadfly." His legacy will endure in the books to come.

Peter Osnos, *Founder and Editor-at-Large*

NOW IT'S YOUR TURN TO MAKE A DIFFERENCE!

We're giving you a **$15 philanthropic gift code** to help the classroom of your choice. Just go to www.DonorsChoose.org/Superman and pick a classroom you want to help. At checkout, enter this code: **92PQYVFN** There are no strings attached.

When I first saw *Waiting for "Superman,"* I was outraged and inspired. Outraged over the thousands of students each year that are let down by public education in this country. Inspired by the glimmers of hope I saw in the teachers who encourage students to think big, who put in extra hours to make sure their classes succeed, and who are so dedicated to their students they spend their own money on classroom supplies.

It is for these teachers and students that I started DonorsChoose.org, an online nonprofit that enables anyone to connect to a public school classroom in a personal and direct way. In the last ten years, we've connected hundreds of thousands of individuals with classrooms, providing resources and materials to over 3 million students.

And now you can make an immediate difference, too. Thanks to the generosity of the Pershing Square Foundation, you can apply $15 to the classroom project that most inspires you. Just visit **www.DonorsChoose.org/Superman** to redeem your gift code.

Thank you on behalf of students and teachers everywhere,

Charles Best

Charles Best, Founder and CEO, DonorsChoose.org